Anthony Quinn

Consulting Editors

Hispanics of Achievement

Anthony Quinn

Melissa Amdur

Chelsea House Publishers
New York   Philadelphia

CHELSEA HOUSE PUBLISHERS

Editor-in-Chief: Richard S. Papale
Executive Managing Editor: Karyn Gullen Browne
Copy Chief: Philip Koslow
Picture Editor: Adrian G. Allen
Art Director: Nora Wertz
Manufacturing Director: Gerald Levine
Systems Manager: Lindsey Ottman
Production Coordinator: Marie Claire Cebrián-Ume

Hispanics of Achievement
Senior Editor: John W. Selfridge

Staff for ANTHONY QUINN
Deputy Copy Chief: Margaret Dornfeld
Designer: Robert Yaffe
Picture Researcher: Nisa Rauschenberg
Cover Illustration: Patty Olean

3 5 7 9 8 6 4 2

Library of Congress Cataloging-in-Publication Data
Amdur, Melissa.
  Anthony Quinn/Melissa Amdur.
    p. cm.—(Hispanics of achievement)
  Includes bibliographical references and index.
  Summary: Discusses the life and career of the Mexican American
actor who has starred in such movies as "Viva Zapata," "Lawrence of
Arabia," and "The Shoes of the Fisherman."
  ISBN 0-7910-1251-4
      0-7910-1278-6 (pbk.)
  1. Quinn, Anthony—Juvenile literature. 2. Motion picture actors
and actresses—United States—Biography—Juvenile literature. [1.
Quinn, Anthony. 2. Actors and actresses. 3. Mexican Americans—
Biography.] I. Title. II. Series.
PN2287.Q5A75 1993   92-19980
791.43'028'092—dc20   CIP
  [B]   AC

Contents

Hispanics of Achievement

Joan Baez
Mexican-American folksinger

Rubén Blades
Panamanian lawyer and entertainer

Jorge Luis Borges
Argentine writer

Juan Carlos
King of Spain

Pablo Casals
Spanish cellist and conductor

Miguel de Cervantes
Spanish writer

Cesar Chavez
Mexican-American labor leader

El Cid
Spanish military leader

Roberto Clemente
Puerto Rican baseball player

Salvador Dalí
Spanish painter

Plácido Domingo
Spanish singer

Gloria Estefan
Cuban-American singer

Gabriel García Márquez
Colombian writer

Pancho Gonzales
Mexican-American tennis player

Francisco José de Goya
Spanish painter

Frida Kahlo
Mexican painter

José Martí
Cuban revolutionary and poet

Rita Moreno
Puerto Rican singer and actress

Pablo Neruda
Chilean poet and diplomat

Antonia Novello
U.S. surgeon general

Octavio Paz
Mexican poet and critic

Pablo Picasso
Spanish artist

Anthony Quinn
Mexican-American actor

Oscar de la Renta
Dominican fashion designer

Diego Rivera
Mexican painter

Linda Ronstadt
Mexican-American singer

Antonio López de Santa Anna
Mexican general and politician

George Santayana
Spanish philosopher and poet

Andrés Segovia
Spanish guitarist

Junípero Serra
Spanish missionary and explorer

Lee Trevino
Mexican-American golfer

Diego Velázquez
Spanish painter

Pancho Villa
Mexican revolutionary

CHELSEA HOUSE PUBLISHERS

INTRODUCTION

Hispanics of Achievement

Rodolfo Cardona

The Spanish language and many other elements of Spanish culture are present in the United States today and have been since the country's earliest beginnings. Some of these elements have come directly from the Iberian Peninsula; others have come indirectly, by way of Mexico, the Caribbean basin, and the countries of Central and South America.

Spanish culture has influenced America in many subtle ways, and consequently many Americans remain relatively unaware of the extent of its impact. The vast majority of them recognize the influence of Spanish culture in America, but they often do not realize the great importance and long history of that influence. This is partly because Americans have tended to judge the Hispanic influence in the United States in statistical terms rather than to look closely at the ways in which individual Hispanics have profoundly affected American culture. For this reason, it is fitting that Americans obtain more than a passing acquaintance with the origins of these Spanish cultural elements and gain an understanding of how they have been woven into the fabric of American society.

It is well documented that Spanish seafarers were the first to explore and colonize many of the early territories of what is today called the United States of America. For this reason, students of geography discover Hispanic names all over the map of the United States. For instance, the Strait of Juan de Fuca was named after the Spanish explorer who first navigated the waters of the Pacific Northwest; the names of states such as Arizona (arid zone), Montana (mountain), Florida (thus named because it was reached on Easter Sunday, which in Spanish is called the feast of Pascua Florida), and California (named after a fictitious land in one of the first and probably the most popular among the Spanish novels of chivalry, *Amadis of Gaul*) are all derived from Spanish; and there are numerous mountains, rivers, canyons, towns, and cities with Spanish names throughout the United States.

Not only explorers but many other illustrious figures in Spanish history have helped define American culture. For example, the 13th-century king of Spain, Alfonso X, also known as the Learned, may be unknown to the majority of Americans, but his work on the codification of Spanish law has greatly influenced the evolution of American law, particularly in the jurisdictions of the Southwest. For this contribution a statue of him stands in the rotunda of the Capitol in Washington, D.C. Likewise, the name Diego Rivera may be unfamiliar to most Americans, but this Mexican painter influenced many American artists whose paintings, commissioned during the Great Depression and the New Deal era of the 1930s, adorn the walls of government buildings throughout the United States. In recent years the contributions of Puerto Ricans, Mexicans, Mexican Americans (Chicanos), and Cubans in American cities such as Boston, Chicago, Los Angeles, Miami, Minneapolis, New York, and San Antonio have been enormous.

The importance of the Spanish language in this vast cultural complex cannot be overstated. Spanish, after all, is second only to English as the most widely spoken of Western languages within the United States as well as in the entire world. The popularity of the Spanish language in America has a long history.

In addition to Spanish exploration of the New World, the great Spanish literary tradition served as a vehicle for bringing the language and culture to America. Interest in Spanish literature in America began when English immigrants brought with them translations of Spanish masterpieces of the Golden Age. As early as 1683, private libraries in Philadelphia and Boston contained copies of the first picaresque novel, *Lazarillo de Tormes,* translations of Francisco de Quevedo's *Los Sueños,* and copies of the immortal epic of reality and illusion *Don Quixote,* by the great Spanish writer Miguel de Cervantes. It would not be surprising if Cotton Mather, the arch-Puritan, read *Don Quixote* in its original Spanish, if only to enrich his vocabulary in preparation for his writing *La fe del cristiano en 24 artículos de la Institución de Cristo, enviada a los españoles para que abran sus ojos* (The Christian's Faith in 24 Articles of the Institution of Christ, Sent to the Spaniards to Open Their Eyes), published in Boston in 1699.

Over the years, Spanish authors and their works have had a vast influence on American literature—from Washington Irving, John Steinbeck, and Ernest Hemingway in the novel to Henry Wadsworth Longfellow and Archibald MacLeish in poetry. Such important American writers as James Fenimore Cooper, Edgar Allan Poe, Walt Whitman, Mark Twain, and Herman Melville all owe a sizable debt to the Spanish literary tradition. Some writers, such as Willa Cather and Maxwell Anderson, who explored Spanish themes they came into contact with in the American Southwest and Mexico, were influenced less directly but no less profoundly.

Important contributions to a knowledge of Spanish culture in the United States were also made by many lesser known individuals—teachers, publishers, historians, entrepreneurs, and

others—with a love for Spanish culture. One of the most signif-
icant of these contributions was made by Abiel Smith, a Harvard
College graduate of the class of 1764, when he bequeathed stock
worth $20,000 to Harvard for the support of a professor of French
and Spanish. By 1819 this endowment had produced enough income to appoint a professor, and the philologist and humanist
George Ticknor became the first holder of the Abiel Smith Chair,
which was the very first endowed Chair at Harvard University.
Other illustrious holders of the Smith Chair would include the
poets Henry Wadsworth Longfellow and James Russell Lowell.

A highly respected teacher and scholar, Ticknor was also a
collector of Spanish books, and as such he made a very special
contribution to America's knowledge of Spanish culture. He was
instrumental in amassing for Harvard libraries one of the first and
most impressive collections of Spanish books in the United States.
He also had a valuable personal collection of Spanish books and
manuscripts, which he bequeathed to the Boston Public Library.

With the creation of the Abiel Smith Chair, Spanish language
and literature courses became part of the curriculum at Harvard,
which also went on to become the first American university to offer
graduate studies in Romance languages. Other colleges and univer-
sities throughout the United States gradually followed Harvard's
example, and today Spanish language and culture may be studied
at most American institutions of higher learning.

No discussion of the Spanish influence in the United States,
however brief, would be complete without a mention of the
Spanish influence on art. Important American artists such as John
Singer Sargent, James A. M. Whistler, Thomas Eakins, and Mary
Cassatt all explored Spanish subjects and experimented with
Spanish techniques. Virtually every serious American artist living
today has studied the work of the Spanish masters as well as the
great 20th-century Spanish painters Salvador Dalí, Joan Miró,
and Pablo Picasso.

The most pervasive Spanish influence in America, however, has probably been in music. Compositions such as Leonard Bernstein's *West Side Story*, the Latinization of William Shakespeare's *Romeo and Juliet* set in New York's Puerto Rican quarter, and Aaron Copland's *Salon Mexico* are two obvious examples. In general, one can hear the influence of Latin rhythms—from tango to mambo, from guaracha to salsa—in virtually every form of American music.

This series of biographies, which Chelsea House has published under the general title HISPANICS OF ACHIEVEMENT, constitutes further recognition of—and a renewed effort to bring forth to the consciousness of America's young people—the contributions that Hispanic people have made not only in the United States but throughout the civilized world. The men and women who are featured in this series have attained a high level of accomplishment in their respective fields of endeavor and have made a permanent mark on American society.

The title of this series must be understood in its broadest possible sense: The term *Hispanics* is intended to include Spaniards, Spanish Americans, and individuals from many countries whose language and culture have either direct or indirect Spanish origins. The names of many of the people included in this series will be immediately familiar; others will be less recognizable. All, however, have attained recognition within their own countries, and often their fame has transcended their borders.

The series HISPANICS OF ACHIEVEMENT thus addresses the attainments and struggles of Hispanic people in the United States and seeks to tell the stories of individuals whose personal and professional lives in some way reflect the larger Hispanic experience. These stories are exemplary of what human beings can accomplish, often against daunting odds and by extraordinary personal sacrifice, where there is conviction and determination. Fray Junípero Serra, the 18th-century Spanish Franciscan missionary, is one such individual. Although in very poor health, he devoted the last 15 years of his life to the foundation of missions throughout California—then a mostly unsettled expanse of land—in an effort to bring a better life to Native Americans through the cultivation of crafts and animal husbandry. An example from recent times, the Mexican-American labor leader Cesar Chavez has battled bitter opposition and made untold personal sacrifices in his effort to help poor agricultural workers who have been exploited for decades on farms throughout the Southwest.

The talent with which each one of these men and women may have been endowed required dedication and hard work to develop and become fully realized. Many of them have enjoyed rewards for their efforts during their own lifetime, whereas others have died poor and unrecognized. For some it took a long time to achieve their goals, for others success came at an early age, and for still others the struggle continues. All of them, however, stand out as people whose lives have made a difference, whose achievements we need to recognize today and should continue to honor in the future.

Anthony Quinn

The Mexican-American actor Anthony Quinn won the Oscar for Best Supporting Actor in 1953 for his performance in the film Viva Zapata! *For Quinn, receiving the award was a great honor, and with characteristic humility he said, "I'm terribly surprised. I didn't think I had a chance."*

CHAPTER ONE

Viva Quinn!

The 25th annual motion picture Academy Awards ceremonies, scheduled for March 19, 1953, promised to be Hollywood's biggest social event of the year. Understandably, the Oscar presentations caused a commotion every year in Hollywood, the entertainment capital of the world. But that year, Tinsel Town was buzzing even more than usual because these ceremonies would be the first to be televised—broadcast live from Los Angeles and New York simultaneously.

Comedian Bob Hope was to host the affair at Hollywood's RKO Pantages Theater, which was decorated with pots of shocking pink azaleas, imitation marble columns, and an enormous blue birthday cake ringed by neon-lighted Oscars that glowed brightly on cue every time an award was announced. In New York City, the awards would be presented at NBC's Century Theater, and the actor Conrad Nagel was to preside over them.

Televising the presentations had opened up a new chapter in the history of the Oscars, because suddenly everyone who owned a television set, that brand-new diversion, could witness the reactions of the stars as they won or lost the award that had come to mean so much to performers and public alike. As Hope quipped at the start of the show, "Keep your eyes on the losers. You'll see great under-standing, great sportsmanship—great acting."

The Oscar earned its strange name under typically humorous Hollywood circumstances. Cedric Gibbons, the art director respon-sible for designing the gold-plated nude man plunging a sword into a reel of film, left a copy of the statuette in the offices of the Academy of Motion Pictures Arts and Sciences. A young employee named Margaret Herrick happened upon the award and exclaimed in surprise, "Why, he looks just like my Uncle Oscar!" The story made its way to a reporter, and the rest is history.

The competition was fierce in 1953—the year before had seen plenty of blockbuster films, produced by Hollywood's most capable studios. Movies such as *The Greatest Show on Earth*, which featured the rough-and-tumble pageantry of the circus world, and *High Noon*, a suspenseful western drama, vied for the top honor of Best Film. Actors Marlon Brando and Gary Cooper battled for the Best Actor prize.

Also among the stellar competitors was another Hollywood favorite, finally enjoying the recognition he so richly deserved with an Oscar nomination for Best Supporting Actor. Anthony Quinn, the versatile character player, was perched on the brink of super-stardom for his role as Eufemio Zapata, brother of the Mexican revolutionary Emiliano Zapata, played by Marlon Brando, in *Viva Zapata!*

But would the Academy of Motion Pictures Arts and Sciences give the much-sought-after award to Quinn? With other Best Sup-porting Actor nominees including Richard Burton and Arthur Hunnicutt, two well-respected performers who had moved smooth-ly into the leading-man roles that Quinn had been seeking for years, the decision was by no means clear cut. Quinn's swarthy, exotic looks had led him to parts that were meaty but often outside the mainsteam and rarely very romantic.

Finally, the much-anticipated moment arrived. Greer Garson, an actress who had been honored in 1942 with an Oscar for Best Actress, made her way to the podium of the Pantages Theater to present the award for Best Supporting Actor. The hushed crowd

In 1936, Quinn (left) played a Native American in The Plainsman, *which starred Gary Cooper (center). The movie was an important one for Quinn: it was his first appearance in a major motion picture, and he met his future wife, Katherine De Mille, on the set.*

waited as she tore open the large white envelope. "And the winner is . . . Mr. Anthony Quinn for *Viva Zapata!*" The applause was deafening as the film community paid their respects to a man often called "the hardest-working actor in Hollywood."

But where was Quinn? True to his reputation, he had been unable to attend the awards ceremony that night because he was

Katherine Quinn accepts the Oscar for Best Supporting Actor on behalf of her husband, Anthony Quinn, who was making a movie in Mexico and was not able to be at the March 19 ceremony in Hollywood. The actress Greer Garson (left), a 1942 Oscar winner, presented the award that evening.

busy filming a new movie in Mexico with his old friend Gary Cooper, who had himself received the award for Best Actor that night. Quinn's wife, Katherine, graciously accepted the Oscar on her husband's behalf, gasping in a surprised voice, "I can hardly believe I'm here!"

When Quinn received the news of his award at his Cuernavaca hotel, he found it incredible that he should be honored along with Cooper, who had starred in Quinn's first major film appearance, *The Plainsman*, some 16 years before. Quinn expressed his delight in his first statement to the press: "Frankly, I'm terribly surprised. I didn't think I had a chance." He then joked with reporters, saying that he was absolutely thrilled about winning the Oscar "because my kids won't think I'm just another bum. Now they'll know what I do for a living!"

Even though he had reached a point in his career that allowed him to accept such an honor with as much humor as awe, his private feelings were shared by those who knew him best. To have won that Oscar was an awfully long way for a poor and hungry boy from Mexico to have come.

Quinn in a scene from the 1937 movie The Last Train from Madrid. *That year the future began to look very bright for the young actor: he signed a contract with Paramount Studios and on October 21 married Katherine De Mille, the adopted daughter of the acclaimed film director Cecil B. De Mille.*

CHAPTER TWO

The Struggle for Survival

The early years of Anthony Rudolph Oaxaca Quinn's life had the epic quality of some of his movies, involving courage in the face of seemingly insurmountable difficulties and triumphs over adversity.

Quinn's mother, Manuela Oaxaca, was reputedly descended from a long line of Aztec royalty. His father, Frank Quinn, a half-Irish, half-Mexican adventurer, fought bravely for Francisco Villa, the Mexican outlaw-revolutionary also known as Pancho Villa. Seventeen-year-old Manuela Oaxaca was newly married and pregnant, living in Chihuahua, Mexico, when Frank, 20, disappeared into the desert hills with Pancho Villa's army to battle the government of President Porfirio Díaz. Anthony was born at dawn on April 21, 1915, while his father was far from their small town. A geranium plant belonging to Manuela had bloomed in the night, the red blossoms foretelling, according to an ancient local legend, the birth of a boy.

It was several months before Frank Quinn returned to his family, only to leave again, this time for the United States. With her

Anthony Quinn was born in Chihuahua, a small Mexican village, in 1915. While Anthony was a child, his father, a soldier and migrant worker, spent long periods away from home. Eventually the family traveled to the United States and settled in East Los Angeles.

husband gone and the fighting in the Mexican countryside intensifying, Manuela began to fear for her life and that of her son. Flight seemed the only solution; it was simply too risky to wait for her husband's return.

Carrying her baby on her back, Manuela headed north on foot, leaving at night to avoid the roving bands of soldiers that terrorized the countryside. Manuela and her son made the next leg of their journey as stowaways on a train, hidden beneath a pile of coal. Manuela was so poor she could not afford the fare to the Mexican border town of Juárez, but a kindly train engineer had offered them safe passage as long as they remained buried in the coal that was used to fuel the train's steam engine.

In Juárez, Manuela and baby Anthony were reunited with Frank Quinn, who had been traveling back and forth across the U.S.-Mexican border to get work. A year later, Manuela gave birth to a baby girl, whom the Quinns named Stella. For the next few years the Quinn family was on the move, along with Anthony's paternal grandmother, Sabina, traveling to wherever work was available.

Usually they were employed as migrant farmworkers, picking fruit and vegetables for low wages and living in workers' housing. Although Anthony was only four years old, he worked alongside his parents and grandmother every day in the hot fields from dawn until dusk. When they had saved enough money to travel to California, they settled in East Los Angeles, a largely Mexican neighborhood plagued by poverty and crime, and Anthony began going to school.

Quinn later recalled this period in his life: "When we were living . . . on the east side of Los Angeles, we lived in a perpetual earthquake. Trains roared by a few yards from our house. . . . Everything in the house rattled, including our teeth." A bridge running past their front yard was noisy with streetcar traffic, and the view from their windows was so desolate that Frank Quinn painted them over with imaginary scenes of mountains, lakes, and pastures.

Frank Quinn found a job with the Selig film studio, caring for the animals the company used in its movies and doing maintenance work on sets and props. He also got his son a job imitating a bear cub for a sequence in a jungle movie, but Anthony never got to play the role: the night before filming was set to begin, the boy became ill, and the part was given to a cousin who was roughly the same age. Recovering quickly from his sickness and his disappointment, Anthony returned to his usual work, selling newspapers and shining shoes. Then, on January 10, 1926, tragedy struck the Quinn household.

The evening had been a pleasant one for Anthony and his family, who had thrown a small party for some friends. When their guests began to leave, it was discovered that their car would not start without a push. Frank Quinn offered to help, and while he was pushing another car struck him, killing him instantly. Manuela could not afford to buy a proper grave marker for her husband, so Anthony, who was only 11 when his father died, crafted one himself and planted it firmly in the grass at his father's grave.

After his father's death, Anthony attended school only sporadically because he had to help support the family. He took whatever odd jobs he could find, but there was an economic depression in the United States during the late 1920s and 1930s, and work was scarce, especially for immigrants. There had been a large influx of Mexicans into the southwestern United States, and with jobs growing scarcer for everyone, resentment and prejudice toward the recent immigrants was widespread.

Anthony was lucky to find work as an electrician's helper, as water boy for the men working on the Los Angeles sewer system, and cleaning up slop from a local slaughterhouse. He also discovered he had an artistic talent that would never cease to be important in his life, and thought of a way to use it to supplement his income. As he later remembered, "I was very good at drawing. I began to copy photographs of famous actors. I did them in Crayola colors. I started to mail the drawings to every important star in Hollywood. I waited for the money to start pouring in. . . . Finally one letter arrived. It was from Douglas Fairbanks. The note merely said, 'Thanks,' but he had enclosed a ten dollar bill. No one else wrote me."

A hunger march on the streets of Los Angeles during the Great Depression of the 1930s, when in the aftermath of the stock market crash of 1929, businesses closed, and millions of Americans were unemployed. At the height of the depression some 12 million American workers lost their jobs.

During the 1930s, Quinn met Aimee Semple McPherson, the flamboyant Pentecostal preacher who in 1927 founded the International Church of the Foursquare Gospel, which he joined. Quinn worked to spread McPherson's Christian fundamentalist message, which attracted thousands of followers.

Also during this period, Anthony met a woman whom he has since referred to as his greatest influence, a woman so magnetic and compelling that his later encounters with the most beautiful leading ladies of Hollywood paled in comparison. Her name was Aimee Semple McPherson, and she became known for the religious organization she founded and the rousing sermons she gave across the United States. Anthony had been raised a devout Roman Catholic, but McPherson's Protestant message of belief in the loving ways of Jesus Christ appealed to him so much that he became involved in her organization, the International Church of the Foursquare Gospel.

As Quinn tells the story, "I started going out into the street, playing my saxophone with three or four of the younger people. We'd stand on corners and play hymns. Crowds would invariably gather round and we would take turns preaching, mostly in Spanish." Quinn often credits his powerful and passionate speaking style to this early, very formative experience. He later trained for the priesthood, but as he once remembered, "the trappings and pomp made me revolt. The simple truths of the Church, which are a pretty good menu for the spiritually hungry, were hidden by the rules."

In the summer of his 14th year, Anthony picked apricots with a group of migrant workers. An apricot ranch owner quickly recognized Anthony's desire to succeed and put him to work as foreman, responsible for supervising more than 150 pickers. The money he made in that one summer allowed the Quinns to live relatively well for a while and gave Anthony time to return to school.

At 15, while a senior at Belvedere Junior High School, Anthony dropped out once again and, claiming that he was 18 years old, landed a well-paying job at a mattress factory. Though Quinn admits it was his favorite job among the many he had held during his teenage years, it came to an abrupt end one afternoon: "I was walking down the alleyway between the assembly lines, [and] I felt a heavy hand on my shoulder. When I turned around I knew who it was. That sneaky face could belong to no one other than my truant officer. My employees must have been surprised to see their foreman being dragged off to school by the scruff of his neck. I wish I could have made a more dignified exit."

By the time he was 16, Anthony stood six feet two inches tall and was blessed with a strong constitution. Believing that with his size and strength he could succeed at boxing, he joined a team of

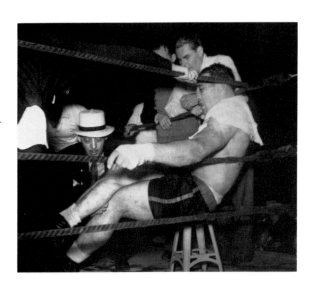

The former heavyweight boxing champion Primo Carnera in his corner during a bout with Leroy Haynes in 1936. For a time, Quinn worked as Carnera's sparring partner and tried to launch a boxing career of his own, but he lacked the killer instinct necessary for success in the ring.

young welterweights under the tutelage of Pop Foster, a well-known trainer and promoter. Anthony's main job was to act as a sparring partner for other up-and-coming boxers and, occasionally, professionals such as Primo Carnera, a four-time heavyweight champion who stood six feet five inches tall and weighed 270 pounds.

Foster, who recognized that Anthony had talent as a sparring partner, arranged for him to fight fast, mean opponents in matches called "smokers." He was paid well for fighting in these exhibition matches, but it soon became apparent that Anthony could not bring himself to deliver a knockout punch. Seeing that Anthony lacked the killer instinct necessary to become a successful prizefighter, Foster advised him to give up any thoughts of a future in boxing.

During his foray into the world of boxing, Anthony attended Polytechnic High in Los Angeles, where his love for art resurfaced. In an architecture class during his sophomore year, he designed a supermarket, entered the design in a competition, and won first prize, which included a meeting with the master architect Frank Lloyd Wright. Wright encouraged Anthony to develop his talent for design, but he noticed that the boy had a slight speech defect, one that had gone largely unnoticed for much of his life. Wright left Anthony with the advice that he work on improving his speech, asserting that clear public speaking was an essential tool in achieving success.

Doctors advised Anthony that surgery would be necessary to correct his speech problem. After he had the operation, a simple procedure to sever a flap of skin called the frenulum on the underside of his tongue, he began undergoing speech therapy with a dramatic arts teacher named Katherine Hamil. A friend had told him about a drama school run by Hamil, but he could not afford the cost of classes. So he made arrangements to trade janitorial work around the school in return for the speech lessons, and the arrangement worked out well for both teacher and student.

Hamil's drama school was known for the high quality of its student productions, plays that were often reviewed by powerful people in the theater and film business. After a very brief time at the school, Anthony, who was reciting a dramatic monologue, caught the attention of the school's director, Max Pollock. With Hamil's encouragement, Anthony was offered and accepted the role of Simon, an upper-class young Englishman, in the school's production of playwright Noël Coward's *Hay Fever*. Quinn was amused by the way things happened and once said of his first acting job, "I couldn't figure out what a kid from my background had in common with the English Simon in Coward's play, but I was eager to find out."

Hay Fever received very good notices in the daily trade papers, and Anthony felt he had found his true path. Director Pollock again offered him a part, this one in a play called *The Lower Depths*, written by the Russian Maksim Gorky. For a second time the play, and Anthony's performance in particular, received good reviews. As a result, he was invited to join a separate theater group called the Gateway Players. Shortly after, acting on a tip from a friend, Anthony found himself auditioning for none other than the legendary comedienne Mae West.

Thanks to the actress Mae West, Quinn landed the leading role in Clean Beds, *a play about the legendary actor John Barrymore. Quinn's performance impressed not only the critics but Barrymore himself, who saw the play twice and struck up a friendship with the actor who so ably portrayed him.*

West's films, such as *She Done Him Wrong* and *My Little Chickadee*, the latter with W. C. Fields, were huge successes in their time. Now she was working on a play called *Clean Beds*, a farce about boarding houses, and needed young "Latin types" to fill out the cast. Anthony was only 19 years old, but he claimed he was 22 in order to audition. West suspected that he was younger than he professed to be; and, anyway, she found that he was too youthful in appearance for any of the parts she had to offer. Anthony started to leave the audition, feeling defeated.

On his way out of the theater, however, Anthony noticed a group of actors auditioning for an interesting part modeled after the actor John Barrymore, who was known for his brilliance on stage and his alcoholism offstage. Quinn was an enormous fan of Barrymore's and impulsively asked the director to be allowed to audition for the part. The director was hesitant at first, given the vast differences in age between Anthony and the character, who was supposed to be in his sixties, but finally he relented.

After Anthony's audition, there was applause from a person standing in the back of the auditorium. It was Mae West. So impressed was West with Anthony's portrayal of the Barrymore character that she spoke to the director and got the young actor the part. Makeup would transform him into the 65-year-old man he would play in *Clean Beds*.

The play was warmly received, and Anthony's portrayal of the cantankerous character was singled out by more than just the critics. John Barrymore himself saw the play twice and wanted to meet the actor behind the parody. He and Anthony met, and to the younger actor's great surprise, formed a friendship that would last until Barrymore's death on May 29, 1942. But *Clean Beds* would ultimately mean more to Anthony Quinn than performing with Mae West and befriending the great Barrymore. The play would lead the young man down a glittering path, from the stage to celluloid and back again, and to the heights of success as one of Hollywood's brightest stars.

In several films, Quinn was cast as a Native American. Here he appears in such a role in the 1944 film Buffalo Bill. *Casting by racial stereotype was a common practice in Hollywood during the 1930s and 1940s, and for much of his career Quinn found it difficult to land nonethnic parts.*

CHAPTER THREE

Hollywood Beckons

The success of *Clean Beds* marked a new chapter in Quinn's career, and the high visibility it gave the young actor paid off. Hollywood director Louis Friedlander had come to see the show and was so taken with Quinn's ability that he offered him a small part in the 1936 film *Parole!* Quinn had worked in front of the cameras only once, several years before, when he had taken work for three dollars per day as an extra in *The Milky Way*, a comedy starring Harold Lloyd.

Although Quinn's scene in *Parole!* was only 45 seconds long, Friedlander shot it in a large closeup, which helped put Quinn square in the public eye. The notices for the movie were very good, especially for Quinn. *Variety,* a trade daily, wrote, "We didn't catch the name of the young man we saw on the screen: he didn't say anything, he just laughed, but I think it is a face that we're going to hear from. I called the studio to find out who he was and they told me his name was Anthony Quinn."

*The comic deadpan actor
Harold Lloyd gets a kiss
from Trixie in a scene from
the movie* The Milky Way.
*Quinn appeared in the
1935 film as an extra,
making his debut, albeit
a brief one, before the
cameras.*

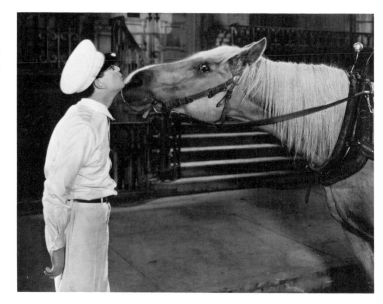

Though Quinn had gained some attention and an enviable
15th billing for *Parole!*, his next two films were not very successful.
In *Sworn Enemy* and *Night Waitress* he played virtually identical
characters, small-time hoods who spent most of their time glower-
ing behind the boss. Quinn received no billing at all for these roles,
and perhaps as a result of the disappointment, he took an impulsive
step away from his blossoming career. No longer so sure of his path,
he packed a small bag with some clothes and a copy of Harry
Kemp's hobo manual *Tramping Through Life* and, with a friend,
hopped on a freight car heading south.

The two young men made their way to Texas, where they found
work digging ditches for 35 cents a day. Then they hit the road
again, eventually winding up south of the border. Then, as Quinn
recalled, "While waiting for a job in Ensenada, Mexico, on one of
the fishing ships that occasionally pulled into port, I picked up a
discarded Los Angeles paper. I read an article that C. B. De Mille
was having difficulty casting a picture called *The Plainsman*. He

couldn't find enough authentic Indians to play some important parts called for by the script." Quinn decided then and there that he had had enough of the hobo's life and hitchhiked back to California with his buddy.

Stopping only in a gas station men's room for a quick shave, Quinn headed directly to Paramount Studios, where auditions for *The Plainsman* were being held. He had the idea that if he could fool De Mille, a director known for such lavish and expensive spectacles as *Samson and Delilah* (1949) and *The Ten Commandments* (1956), into believing he was a full-blooded Cheyenne Indian, he would deserve the part of a warrior chief.

Many humorous anecdotes surround the first meeting of these two men. One story has it that Quinn used a made-up sign language to indicate he could not speak English, that he was conversant only in Cheyenne, to which De Mille responded happily by using sign language right back! The more believable version of the story features a studio lackey who, like Quinn, was Mexican and who for some unknown reason was presumed by studio bigwigs to know Cheyenne. This was definitely not the case, but nevertheless the man was summoned to check the authenticity of Quinn's assertion

The director Cecil B. De Mille (pointing), on the set of The Plainsman. *De Mille directed Quinn in the 1936 film, in which the actor played a Cheyenne chief. It was his first featured movie role.*

that he was 100 percent Cheyenne. Quinn related the story this way in his memoir, *The Original Sin*: "De Mille turned to the Mexican fellow and said, 'See if he can talk Cheyenne.' The Mexican looked at me and made some sounds: 'Xtmas ala huahua?' Clearly phony, so I said, 'Xtmas nana ellahuahua cheriota hodsvi.' He turned to De Mille and said, 'Oh, yes, he speak good Cheyenne.'"

Whatever the exact circumstances were, Quinn managed to bluff his way into the part and was actually required to learn to speak some Cheyenne for a long speech given toward the end of the movie. But Quinn's gutsy, hilarious deception was not the only performance to win him acclaim on and off the studio set. In a display of boldness unrivaled by any other rookie actor before him, Quinn decided to argue against playing the warrior part the way

Quinn (in pinstripes) and his wife, Katherine, with her adoptive parents, Mr. and Mrs. Cecil B. De Mille, in 1937. De Mille had an uneasy rapport with his son-in-law, who struggled to prove that his success as an actor was independent of his family relationship with the great director.

De Mille wanted him to. No one had ever disagreed with De Mille before as to how a scene should be played—certainly not an unknown young actor with virtually no film experience. One of the most powerful directors at Paramount, De Mille could end a career just as quickly as he could launch one.

De Mille loomed large as a Hollywood mogul, but other studio bigwigs such as Louis B. Mayer, head of MGM (Metro-Goldwyn-Mayer), Darryl F. Zanuck, who ran 20th Century Fox, and Jesse Lasky, a part owner of Paramount, were equally typical of the mold. These men maintained absolute control over the production and content of every film that bore their studio's name and were the last word when actors' salaries were at issue. They made all decisions regarding publicity and determined what theaters were appropriate for their films, thereby extending their authority into the realm of the general public. Mayer, Zanuck, and Lasky built their studios into some of the most powerful institutions in the United States. Therefore, few people had the courage to question the decisions these film moguls made, and those who did were usually shown the nearest exit.

The set was silent as the crew awaited the explosion they knew was coming. Sure enough, De Mille erupted in a fit worthy of a California earthquake, but Quinn stood his ground before the director's wrath, receiving a torrent of abuse and threats of immediate banishment from the set. Quinn had to shout to make himself heard, but he insisted that no Indian would do what De Mille had planned. Quinn felt that what De Mille wanted just was not realistic. As he remembers the end of the confrontation, "A hundred and fifty people—the crew, Gary Cooper—held their breath as De Mille and I stared at each other for what seemed like an awfully long time. He suddenly turned around and said, 'The boy's right. We'll change the setup.' And there was a sigh of relief from everybody. I did the scene my way." Quinn became a legend that day; soon all of Hollywood was talking about the brash young actor who had dared to defy De Mille—and who had triumphed.

Quinn (left) appears with Fred MacMurray and Carole Lombard in a scene from the 1937 film Swing High, Swing Low, *in which he played a Panamanian and delivered almost all his lines in Spanish. Quinn was frustrated with such roles because of the racial stereotypes attached to them.*

Yet another event took place on the set of *The Plainsman* that would change the course of Anthony Quinn's life. During his first afternoon on the set he had noticed a lovely young woman with large dark eyes and fine features talking with De Mille during the filming. He assumed, because of her rich brunette coloring, that she was another Indian extra. She was, in fact, De Mille's adopted daughter, Katherine, a young actress in the Paramount studio stable. In a classic case of "love at first sight," she and Quinn were smitten with each other and, after a brief courtship, were married on October 21, 1937. Katherine De Mille's parents had died during her early childhood, and she had become a part of the De Mille family at the age of seven. She made more than 24 movies in her career, which she mostly gave up after her marriage to raise the couple's four children.

The Plainsman brought still more good things Quinn's way. Because of his well-known dispute with De Mille, Quinn attracted the attention of the comedic actress Carole Lombard, a powerful star known for her own outspoken nature. She used her influence to help land Quinn a part in her upcoming film, *Swing High, Swing Low.*

As a young Panamanian who competes with Fred MacMurray for Lombard's love, Quinn spoke mostly Spanish, but the role paid very well—$200 per day. His next film offer came from the director Frank Tuttle, who had not only heard of Quinn's showdown with De Mille but had also seen his performance in *Clean Beds*. The part called for Quinn to play a grass-skirted Hawaiian native in the Bing Crosby comedy *Waikiki Wedding*. Next, Lombard tried to line him up with a major role, recently turned down by the actor George Raft, in a film called *Souls at Sea*, for which Quinn auditioned and was chosen. Unfortunately for Quinn, Raft had a change of heart at the last minute and took the part. The Paramount studio hired Quinn on contract, however, thus placing him among the ranks of movie notables—including Marlene Dietrich, Bing Crosby, and Gloria Swanson—who also had Paramount contracts.

As Quinn's career took off, rumors spread that the actor had married the boss's daughter in order to advance professionally, but this was far from the truth. He was actually quite determined to make it as an actor on his own. He said at the time, "I get along fine with my father-in-law, and I think he likes and respects me. But I didn't want anyone even to think I was marrying into the Royal family for anything more than I got—which was Katherine." Quinn would eventually work on several projects with De Mille but only after he had made a name for himself without any favors from his father-in-law.

Although he eventually overcame the problem of racial stereotypes in Hollywood film casting, Quinn next found himself locked into the role of the villain, particularly in gangster movies. But because he got to work with some of the best directors of the genre, Quinn was glad for the new challenge.

CHAPTER FOUR

On His Own

Quinn appeared in a number of "B" movies along with other actors, such as Anna May Wong and Akim Tamiroff, whose looks made them perfect for "ethnic" roles. These movies were generally made on smaller budgets than those of "A" movies, which starred Hollywood's more popular players. Quinn's heavy jaw and forbidding brow made him an easy choice when gangster or bad-guy parts were being cast. This typecasting discouraged him because it deprived him of decent roles in good movies.

A particular source of frustration for Quinn was that although he was a very handsome, dashing man, he was often considered too dark to play leading roles. Instead he played "bad guys." But at least there was no shortage of villain roles, and Quinn poured his talents into each one, working with some of Hollywood's finest action-film directors, such as Edward Dmytryk, Louis King, and Robert Florey. The B-list melodramas were some of the biggest money-makers on the Paramount lot and, aside from providing Quinn with gainful employment, they taught him a lot about movie acting.

Although Quinn had mostly minor roles in the "B" movies he appeared in, he often dominated his scenes with his powerful presence. In later years, Quinn developed a reputation as an outrageous scene-stealer, prompting stars like Gregory Peck and Jackie Gleason to complain that Quinn managed to overpower them even when he was standing behind them and not saying anything.

One of Quinn's first films as a Paramount contract player was *Daughter of Shanghai*, starring Anna May Wong, a Chinese-born actress. Like Quinn, Wong found that ethnic typecasting prevented her from landing better roles. She and Quinn became close friends on the set of their first film together.

Shortly after making a handful of these low-budget pictures, Quinn was invited to appear in another Cecil B. De Mille production, *The Buccaneer*. Though he wanted the leading role in this pirate epic, Quinn was considered too young to be believable in it

Quinn appeared with the Chinese-American actress Anna May Wong in the 1937 movie Daughter of Shanghai, *and the two quickly became good friends. Like Quinn, Wong was the victim of racial stereotypes that seemed always to dictate which roles she could get and which she could not.*

Cecil B. De Mille (in fedora) directs a scene from the 1939 film Union Pacific,
*the third movie Quinn made with his father-in-law and also the last. That year,
Katherine Quinn gave birth to a son, Christopher.*

and instead was cast as a crew member on the ship of Jean Lafitte.
Then it was back to the Paramount lot to make more "B" movies—
Hunted Men, King of Alcatraz, Television Spy, and *Island of Lost Men.*
Every now and then, Paramount would feature Quinn in one of its
pricier films, such as the Bing Crosby–Bob Hope collaborations
Road to Singapore and *Road to Morocco,* both with Dorothy Lamour.
Quinn also made a third movie with De Mille, *Union Pacific,* the last
the actor would make with his father-in-law.

During the filming of *Union Pacific,* a columnist wrote about
Quinn's having been invited to share De Mille's reserved area for
lunch: "Now that Tony Quinn is the boss's son-in-law, he feels it
beneath him to break bread with the common people on location."

The column was an afront to the man who had worked so hard to avoid being thought of as an opportunist. When his player's contract came up in 1940, Quinn refused to renegotiate it even though the studio's offer was handsome. A player's contract guaranteed a performer a weekly salary whether or not he or she was actually filming a picture. It was a nice safety net to have if offers for parts were not forthcoming. However, Quinn decided not to play it safe but rather to try his luck around the other studios for which he had worked on loan from Paramount.

Christopher Quinn takes direction from his parents in a 1939 family portrait. The boy drowned in a tragic swimming pool accident two years later.

Meanwhile, in 1939, Katherine gave birth to a son, whom the couple named Christopher. The following year, Quinn signed on with Warner Bros. Studios, raising his salary to about $750 a week, three times what he had been earning at Paramount. His first movie for Warner Bros. was *City for Conquest*, starring Jimmy Cagney and featuring Elia Kazan and Arthur Kennedy, two young actors with whom Quinn would remain lifelong friends. Quinn was billed 10th in this fairly successful film and was able to show off his skill as a dancer, as he had earlier done in *Road to Singapore*.

Following *City for Conquest*, Quinn went back to playing gangster roles until he was cast as the vengeful Chief Crazy Horse in the blockbuster film *They Died with Their Boots On*, starring Errol Flynn as General Custer. Custer was the U.S. cavalryman who in 1876 was killed with his entire command by Sioux and Cheyenne Indians on the Little Bighorn River. Even though Quinn was still playing a "character" part, the quality of the movie went a long way toward assuaging some of the dissatisfaction he had felt at not being offered better roles.

Then, on March 15, 1941, a personal tragedy struck the Quinn household. During a party at the De Mille estate, two-year-old Christopher strayed from the family festivities and fell into a swimming pool on a neighboring estate. He drowned before help could arrive. The Quinns had a second child later that year, a girl they named Christina, and subsequently three more children: Kathleen, born in 1942; Duncan, in 1945; and Valentina, in 1952. Family life was very important to Quinn, who over the years gained a reputation for being one of the most devoted family men in Hollywood.

Later in 1941, Quinn was loaned to 20th Century Fox from Warner Bros. to make a film that later became a classic. It was a remake of *Blood and Sand*, a film that originally starred Rudolph Valentino, one of the all-time kings of smoldering passion. The new version featured Tyrone Power in the role of a dashing matador. Quinn played the matador's friend and principal rival in the bull-

Quinn (left) and Tyrone Power play rival matadors in the 1941 remake of Blood and Sand, *which originally starred the silent-film actor Rudolph Valentino. Quinn delivered such a fine performance that more than one critic referred to him as the new Valentino.*

fighting ring and appeared in a scene with the female lead, Rita Hayworth, with whom Quinn shared a dance.

Quinn's bravura elegance brought on instant comparison to the heartthrob Valentino, whose death in 1926 at the age of 31 left thousands of anguished female fans, some so distraught that they committed suicide. The feedback was so positive that Quinn even asked his old friend John Barrymore if he thought pursuing a film project based on Valentino's life would be a good idea. Barrymore did not think it was at all worthwhile because, as Quinn reported, "the old Valentino fans would tear me to pieces, and those who didn't know the famous silent film lover couldn't care less." Quinn gave up on the idea and returned once again to the Paramount studio.

One of the great leading men of silent films, Rudolph Valentino died tragically in 1926 at the age of 31. His death saddened thousands of moviegoers, and some of his female admirers were distraught to the point of attempting suicide. A few succeeded in taking their lives, a few did not.

Quinn next signed a three-year deal with 20th Century Fox. In his first film under this contract he played a pirate in the film *The Black Swan.* For this role Quinn was decked out in typical Hollywood pirate garb and also wore a fuzzy dark wig, a long false scar, and the obligatory eye patch to complete the look. After he finished making this salty yarn, Quinn appeared in a film that would be considered one of the finest of his career and one that has become a modern classic—*The Ox-Bow Incident.*

In *The Ox-Bow Incident,* made in 1943 and starring Dana Andrews and Francis Ford, Quinn played a young Mexican who is unjustly accused of cattle rustling. In one dramatic scene, Quinn's character bravely stands up to an irate lynch mob. Directed by William Wellman, the movie was considered a small but beautifully handled portrait of prejudice and of life in the old West. For Quinn, having known more than his share of prejudice growing up poor and Mexican in Los Angeles, the movie struck a deep chord.

Following this important film, Quinn took on a guts-and-glory war tale called *Guadalcanal Diary*, in which he again played a Mexican, this time a U.S. Marine. The film was a departure from previous studio productions because for the first time (and because of the onset of World War II), Hollywood presented a cross-section of racial types. The idea of "brothers in arms" had not been explored before, and an image of ethnic unity suddenly became fashionable. Quinn received very good notices for his performance as the sole survivor of a patrol unit wiped out during fierce combat.

But for Quinn good roles were still the exception, not the rule, and in his next few films he went back to the same tired ground he had covered earlier in his career, playing Indians and gangsters in a few movies released quickly by the studio to make fast cash. The films were for the most part forgetable, but in one, *Ladies in Washington*, Quinn got his first kissing scene, a breakthrough for the handsome actor who had so far been denied the chance to play a romantic lead. Aside from the kiss, however, the movie went nowhere, and Quinn, in search of more fulfilling parts, began asking to be loaned to a variety of studios. As Quinn recalls, "I have always been in the process of discovering. That's the way it was for me then. I didn't mind playing Indians, but a lot of other parts I was in made me unhappy. I was frequently the leading man's friend or a gangster."

After he had completed his contractual commitments to Fox, Quinn tried his luck with RKO Pictures, working on a series of action movies with stars such as John Wayne and Douglas Fairbanks, Jr. His roles ran the gamut of ethnic heavies, from the evil emir in *Sinbad the Sailor* to a Chinese guerrilla leader in *Back to Bataan*. Quinn remained dissatisfied.

Quinn's last film during this difficult period in his career was made independently and distributed by a company called Allied Artists. It was a low-budget feature called *Black Gold*, in which Quinn starred as an Indian rancher who discovers oil on his property. Quinn's wife, Katherine, also starred in the film, their first and only time together on the big screen.

Made in 1947, *Black Gold* details the rise and fall of a newly made American Indian millionaire as he tries his best to enter the exclusive world of white men by breeding racehorses. Soon after his horse wins the Kentucky Derby, the man becomes ill, and his wife, a well-educated and gentle woman, and his adopted son can only stand by and watch. Although the film went largely unnoticed because of poor distribution and the critics who did see it were not impressed, Quinn felt close to the subject matter, and *Black Gold* remains to this day one of Quinn's personal favorites. Still, the cool reception of the movie did not bode well for the unhappy actor, who realized it was time he got his career moving or else find some other way to make a living.

Looking for new challenges, Quinn took leave from Hollywood moviemaking in 1947 to star in a stage production of The Gentleman from Athens. *After a successful run in Boston, the play opened on Broadway, and it was ravaged by the New York critics, although they praised Quinn's performance.*

CHAPTER FIVE

From Stage to Screen and Back Again

Quinn's chance to revitalize his career came in 1947 with an offer from Sam Wanamaker, who was trying to produce a play called *The Gentleman from Athens*, slated for Broadway. It had been many years since Quinn had done stage work, but after reviewing the script he knew it was a good proposition. The story revolved around an assertive Greek-American politician from Athens, California, who uses questionable methods to get himself elected to Congress. Quinn readily invested $25,000 of his own money—a substantial portion of his savings at the time—to help produce the show, and he threw himself into the lead role.

The Gentleman from Athens opened in Boston for previews, and Quinn received excellent reviews. For example, the critic Eliot Norton wrote, "Mr. Quinn, who was a blanketed Injun and some- times a Maharaja in the movies, until he became a gentleman from Athens, California, is a wow in this show. . . . He is a natural actor and if *The Gentleman from Athens* is a hit, he will take his place among the stars." Unfortunately, the play was not a hit on Broadway. Nevertheless, Quinn was encouraged by the good notices his Boston performances had received and sensed he was on the right track with his return to stage work.

By 1948 scriptwriters were finding an increasingly lucrative market for their work in the television medium. Sales of television sets had been doubling yearly, and it looked as though there would be no turning back from the popularity of home entertainment.

Quinn made his television debut in a special "Philco Playhouse" production, a play called *Pride's Castle*, written by Frank Yerby. Quinn would go on to be involved in a number of television productions during the next two decades, among them the plays *Lights Out* and *House of Dust*, but it was not until the 1970s that he would star in his own series. In the late 1940s, opportunities in television were only beginning to open up, and the exposure was still relatively low for actors who chose to take that route.

Quinn returned to the stage when he got an offer from his old friend Elia Kazan, who had made the transition from acting to directing. Kazan was casting the part of Stanley Kowalski in a production of *A Streetcar Named Desire*. The Tennessee Williams

Marlon Brando and Jessica Tandy starred in the 1947 Broadway production of Tennessee Williams's Streetcar Named Desire. *Quinn replaced Brando when the company went on tour, impressing the critics with a performance that equaled if not surpassed Brando's.*

play was already running on Broadway, starring Marlon Brando and Jessica Tandy as the combative Stanley and Stella, but the touring version would play other American cities, beginning with Chicago. The actress Uta Hagen would play Stella to Quinn's Stanley, and the pair generated the heat and violence that was so integral to the story.

Quinn was a natural choice to play Stanley Kowalski, a swaggering, brutish character with a raw, sensual nature. It was a part that required the kind of magnetism Quinn possessed but had been forced to keep in check for so many of his movie roles. The show was extremely successful around the country; then, in August 1949, Quinn played the role on Broadway, replacing Ralph Meeker, who had replaced Brando. Quinn spent nearly a year and a half performing in *Streetcar*, going on the road with the company again, then returning to Broadway for a special-engagement run. Critics sang the praises of Quinn's Kowalski, most agreeing that he was every bit Brando's equal, if not his superior, in technique and talent.

After his run in *Streetcar* had ended, Quinn explored other stage roles, this time in off-Broadway productions, but in these smaller ventures he found it difficult to match the level of intensity he had experienced doing *Streetcar*. He returned to Hollywood in 1950 and landed a part in a film entitled *The Brave Bulls*, in which he played the manager of a cowardly matador. Quinn has said that he made the movie for "peanuts" because his earning power had plummeted in the time he spent away from the industry. Nevertheless, the film did well and was hailed as one of the best movie portrayals of the spectacle of bullfighting.

Although Quinn had once more captured the attention of the moviegoing public, the stage continued to lure him. When he got an offer to play the part of a film producer in the play *Let Me Hear the Melody*, costarring with Melvyn Douglas and Cloris Leachman, Quinn could not refuse the opportunity. But the play closed soon after it opened, and Quinn decided once more to return to movies.

Quinn as Eufemio, the brother of the Mexican revolutionary Emiliano Zapata, in the 1952 movie Viva Zapata! *Marlon Brando played the lead role, and the novelist John Steinbeck wrote the screenplay for the film. Quinn's performance won him an Oscar for Best Supporting Actor.*

The next film Quinn worked on was *Viva Zapata!* Along with Quinn, the film starred Marlon Brando and was directed by Elia Kazan, two fellow alumni of *A Streetcar Named Desire.* In *Viva Zapata!* Quinn played Eufemio Zapata, the brother of the revolutionary Emiliano, who in 1911 led a movement toward land reforms to benefit the peasants in Mexico. It was indeed ironic that Quinn, a Mexican American, was passed over for the lead in favor of Brando, but their very different styles suited the characters. Quinn's portrayal of Eufemio was wild and woolly; he raged, cajoled, and cavorted, while Brando's Emiliano was silent and taciturn. The following year, Quinn finally received some of the acclaim that was so long overdue when he was presented with an Oscar for his work in the film.

Despite the exposure and recognition the Oscar brought him, Quinn still had trouble getting interesting movie roles. By playing scoundrels and tough guys in fast and furious action movies, Quinn was earning a handsome living, but he desperately wanted a greater challenge than those roles offered. To his dismay, he was still passed over as a leading man in favor of younger, less experienced actors such as Rock Hudson, Jeff Chandler, and John Derek. One reason

Quinn had difficulty getting roles during this period was that he looked ethnic during a time when foreigners were considered suspect.

Relations between the world's two superpowers, the United States and the Soviet Union, had been deteriorating steadily since the end of World War II. The term *cold war* was coined to describe those relations, which were characterized by suspicion and the threat of conflict. The so-called iron curtain had fallen on the Eastern European countries that the Soviet Union had claimed after World War II, and the spread of communism alarmed many Americans. As a result, the fires of a particular brand of paranoia, known as McCarthyism, swept the United States.

The Republican senator from Wisconsin, Joseph McCarthy, knew he could exploit the cold war mentality for his own political gain. A shrewd political zealot, McCarthy played on the fears and anxieties of the cold war, fueling the fires of anticommunism, by waging a highly publicized campaign to expose so-called Communist sympathizers in the United States. To this end, McCarthy made irresponsible and groundless charges against people in government, entertainment, and the media, frequently destroying careers and lives. For a time, anyone McCarthy accused of having Communist ties was blacklisted and thus denied any chance of obtaining work. As the level of paranoia intensified, people throughout the country were caught up in the hysteria, many of them informing on their friends and neighbors. In a very short time, a fear of communism became a fear of anything foreign.

The McCarthy era was a sad time in U.S. history. The U.S. government and the media threw aside the Constitution, and the country plunged into a state of panic. Thankfully, McCarthy brought about his own demise in 1954, when he accused a member of the U.S. military, a man with an untarnished record, of treason. This was more than the Senate could bear, and in December of that year, it voted overwhelmingly to condemn McCarthy, and thereafter his influenced quickly waned. Still, there was no mending the many lives McCarthy had destroyed with his red-baiting.

Many movies of the period reflected the cold war mentality. One such film was *The World in His Arms*, a seafaring tale starring Anthony Quinn as a Portuguese sailor.

Quinn appeared in three hastily made films—*Seminole*, *City Beneath the Sea*, and *East of Sumatra*—and then moved to MGM. In 1953, he appeared in *Ride, Vaquero!*, a film directed by John Farrow, with Ava Gardner and Robert Taylor, then huge box-office draws, and his portrayal of the scheming, conniving José Esqueda received high critical praise. Quinn next worked with Gary Cooper and Barbara Stanwyck in his second MGM film, *Blowing Wild*, also a western. In this stagecoach and sagebrush saga, Quinn plays the unsuspecting husband of a murderous Stanwyck, who pushes him into an oil well so that she can pursue an affair with Cooper. But Quinn wanted more out of performing than just winding up on the wrong side of a gusher, and so he planned his next career move.

Hollywood appeared to be stuck in its own rigid system of defining actors by their appearance and skin color rather than their talents, and although Quinn had got some substantive, even fulfilling roles during the previous three years, he was still often stereotyped and thus limited. Quinn desperately wanted to break down those stereotypes and believed he might do so by choosing his roles differently. He began to accept only what he considered substantive roles, even if his screen time was only minutes long. As a result, his work became challenging, and he came to be respected more as a character actor.

Soon Quinn earned a reputation as a perfectionist because of the intense concentration and care he brought to even the smallest roles. This determination to get it right sometimes led directors to brand him "difficult to work with," because getting to the essence of a part took time. In short, Quinn was evolving into a Method actor, or one who goes through the difficult process of acquiring a complete identification with a character before rendering a portrayal.

During the 1950s, an increasing number of actors, especially in Europe, explored Method acting, a technique originally taught by the Russian stage director Konstantin Stanislavski. They claimed that the technique helped them develop their powers of relaxation, concentration, and memory, dramatically improving their performances. In the United States, the technique was taught by Lee Strasberg and Stella Adler, among others, and the technique could claim such American disciples as James Dean and Marlon Brando, and later, Robert De Niro and Dustin Hoffman.

While the finer points of this very demanding technique went largely unappreciated by American directors, filmmakers in Europe embraced Method acting as part of the trend toward realism. The Italian film director Roberto Rossellini is widely credited with having begun the movement with his post–World War II masterpiece *Open City*. The film's lack of staging, unstudied camera work, and use of nonprofessional actors all added up to a kind of realism never before seen on the movie screen. Other European directors—particularly the Italians Vittorio De Sica and Federico Fellini—participated in this movement. A new wave of serious filmmaking had taken hold across the Atlantic, and Quinn knew that if he wanted to scale the heights of his art, he would find the opportunity not in Hollywood but in Europe.

Frustrated by the restrictions imposed on actors by the Hollywood studios and aware of a new and exciting cinema emerging in France and Italy during the early 1950s, Quinn decided to go to Europe to explore new possibilities. He left Hollywood for Italy in 1953.

Quinn and Italian actress Sophia Loren in a scene from the 1958 film
The Black Orchid. *Quinn's work in Italian film during the 1950s*
allowed him to grow as an artist in ways his work in Hollywood never did.

CHAPTER SIX

Moviemaking Italian Style

In early 1953, Quinn flew to Italy, a country that was to have a profound influence on both his career and his personal life. While his first few Italian films were not of the highest caliber, they nonetheless established Quinn as a budding international star and finally allowed him to break through the old Hollywood barriers he had been up against for so long. He was also making movies at a tremendous speed, appearing in five films in only 11 months.

One of these films was *Donne Prohibite* (Forbidden Women), which provided Quinn with an introduction to the actress Giulietta Masina and her husband, the director Federico Fellini. Fellini appreciated the actor's work and asked Quinn to look over the script for his latest project, a film entitled *La Strada* (The Road), and to consider appearing in it. Quinn had seen Fellini's first feature, *I Vittelone* (The Hustlers), and had recognized it as a work of genius. After reading the script for *La Strada*, he agreed to play the strongman Zampano, a cruel and brutish carnival performer who victimizes his feebleminded assistant, played by Masina.

The Italian actress Giulietta Masina in a scene from La Strada, *directed by her husband, Federico Fellini. Soon after Masina introduced Quinn to Fellini in 1954, the director handed him a script and offered him a part in the film.*

When it premiered in the United States, *La Strada* quickly became one of the most talked-about films of the year, and Quinn's performance was a large part of the film's success. Quinn was so engaged by the complex and lonely character of Zampano that his rendering is one of the most powerful portraits of sadness on film. Especially remarkable is Quinn's work in the film's final scenes, when Zampano's uncontrollable rage leads to tragedy. This emotional climax secured Quinn a place alongside the greatest film actors of all time.

Quinn acknowledged his debt to Fellini for teaching him some essential lessons in the craft of moviemaking. A small example of Fellini's relentless pursuit of excellence was the painstaking four hours it took to select the cigar box Zampano would carry with him in the movie. Quinn and Fellini examined more than 300 boxes before settling on a worn and battered tin case. Of the experience, Quinn has said: "People have the impression that the great Italian directors Fellini or [Michelangelo] Antonioni perform their . . . miracles by osmosis. It isn't so. They do it by a steady attention to detail." The making of *La Strada* was exhilarating for Fellini also, and he was happy to have worked with Quinn, whom he called "the kind of actor who enables a director to make a great picture."

Shortly after *La Strada* was completed, Quinn said to an interviewer that *La Strada* was "probably the one picture that had the greatest effect on my life." Indeed, the success of *La Strada* sent Quinn and his career off on a whirlwind course of intercontinental travel. Although he had designed and built a home for his family in the California town of Ojai, owned real estate in Connecticut and New York, and kept an apartment in Paris, Quinn had fallen under the spell of Italy and decided to rent a villa there for himself and his family. The country's magnificent scenery, ancient ruins, and relaxed way of life had all conspired to make Quinn feel as though he had found a new home. Quinn's wife and children joined him, flying back and forth between Italy and the United States as his schedule demanded.

Quinn as the brutish carnival performer Zampano in Fellini's La Strada. *Immediately upon the film's release, the critics declared it a cinematic masterpiece, and Quinn's performance in it earned him international recognition as one of the world's finest actors.*

What followed was an exhausting but exciting time for Quinn, who was making European and American films one after the other. In 1954, he starred in *The Long Wait*, adapted from a hard-boiled mystery novel by Mickey Spillane. Then it was back to Italy for the filming of *Attila the Hun*, an epic based on the life of the 5th-century warrior Attila. In 1955, Quinn returned to Mexico City to make *The Magnificent Matador*, in which he starred alongside Maureen O'Hara. Then, back in Hollywood, he starred in *The Naked Street*, a gangster film that also featured Anne Bancroft as Quinn's younger sister, and a big-screen adventure called *Seven Cities of Gold*.

Quinn's next movie was *Lust for Life*. Directed by Vincente Minnelli— who won an Oscar for Best Director for the film *Gigi*— and based on the novel by the best-selling author Irving Stone, *Lust for Life*, a biography of the Dutch painter Vincent van Gogh, was expected to be a big hit. Van Gogh, born in 1853, was a failed art dealer and a missionary before he discovered painting. Although subject to fits of madness and depression, he painted hundreds of canvases and came to be considered one of the 19th century's great

Quinn as the French painter Paul Gauguin in the movie Lust for Life, *based on the life of the Dutch artist Vincent van Gogh. Although he was only on screen for six minutes, Quinn delivered a powerful performance that in 1956 won him his second Oscar for Best Supporting Actor.*

artists. Kirk Douglas, who was best known for his starring role in *Spartacus* and who bore an uncanny resemblance to the painter, was lined up to play van Gogh. Director Minnelli asked Quinn to read for the part of the compulsively driven artist Paul Gauguin, a friend of van Gogh's who became notorious for leaving his wife and family to pursue his painting on the South Pacific island of Tahiti. The prospect of playing the role of Gauguin excited Quinn, and although the part was a small one, Quinn threw himself into the role. Of his intensive preparation for the film, Quinn has said, "As Gauguin, I had to do more than just carry paintings. I had to go through the same soul-searching he did before he left his wife and children. I myself was almost 40. I had four children. Was I happy? Did I give a damn what people thought? When I found myself uncaringly walking into a French village with flowers I'd picked, I knew I had established contact with the painter."

For his performance in *Lust for Life*, Quinn won a second Oscar for Best Supporting Actor. He had appeared for only six minutes in the film, the least amount of time spent on screen by any award winner on record, but in that six minutes, he had managed to get the Oscar nod over his fellow nominees—Mickey Rooney, Anthony Perkins, and Robert Stack—all fine actors with strong performances that year. In his acceptance speech at the awards ceremony, Quinn said that he was grateful for the award but that in his view he was never in competition with the other nominees. His only competitor, he said, was himself. He set his own standards of excellence, and with each new role he struggled to meet them.

At the 1956 Academy Awards, Quinn was recognized yet again for his accomplishments. That year, a new award category—Best Foreign Film—was created, and of the five foreign films nominated that year, *La Strada* took top honors. Thus Quinn, whose performace was crucial to the film's success, was again thrust into the limelight.

With the 1956 Academy Awards, Quinn had attained superstardom, but he was not content to rest on past achievements.

Rather, he began to explore other aspects of the movie business, hoping to gain greater control over his choice of material and the film production process. He had already set up a production company with Kirk Douglas, and although no projects emerged from it, the company provided an active breeding ground for new ideas. Production companies initiated by actors have since become commonplace, but in the late 1950s the concept was relatively new, representing a daring alternative to the overly protective studios. To the maverick Quinn, the idea of greater independence was irresistible.

Another of the independent projects that occupied Quinn toward the latter half of the 1950s sprang from the actor's generosity. Knowing well the feelings of insecurity and disappointment that plagued young actors just starting out, he decided to rent a space above a retail store in Hollywood and hold free acting classes there. Quinn invited other experienced actors to join him in offering advice to budding performers. Of this project Quinn said, "Now I'm in the position to lend encouragement to beginners and nothing makes me prouder." The school was popular, and many of Quinn's students—such as Paul Newman, Joanne Woodward, and Irene Pappas—went on to become successful actors.

In his next film, *The Man from Del Rio,* Quinn starred as a Mexican gunslinger who is suddenly made the sheriff of a small Texas town. The movie was decidedly low budget, and the studio did not spend much time or money promoting it, but Quinn was excited about the role. "Because my part was a friendless outlaw with no sense of responsibility," he later said, "a man full of racial prejudice . . . I felt it was something I wanted to make a comment on."

Westerns were very much in fashion in Hollywood during the late 1950s, and television was setting the standard for a new kind of gritty realism. Quinn, of course, benefited greatly from this interest, having played cowboys and Indians since the beginning of his career. In 1957, Quinn appeared in two westerns—*The Ride Back* and *The Long Trail.*

Offers to play romantic leads continued to pass Quinn by, but this was beginning to matter less—his main interest now lay elsewhere. Quinn had come to enjoy the challenge of portraying complex, unusual, even ugly characters and even to prefer these to more conventional roles. For Quinn, playing a character meant getting inside the person and exploring his psyche, and he found the dark, troubled characters fascinating. He became obsessed with the idea of imparting beauty to grotesque figures and of garnering sympathy for characters that on the surface seemed monstrous. It was the role of Quasimodo, the misshapen bell ringer in Victor Hugo's tragic tale *The Hunchback of Notre Dame,* that provided a channel for Quinn's new artistic passion.

Quasimodo was already a familiar film character, having been portrayed previously by the great actors Lon Chaney in 1923 and

Quinn as the grotesque Quasimodo in the 1956 remake of the film The Hunchback of Notre Dame, *based on the novel by the French writer Victor Hugo. The film received good reviews in France, where it was produced, but it went mostly unnoticed in the United States.*

Charles Laughton in 1940. When French director Jean Delannoy decided to do yet another rendition, he invited Quinn to play Quasimodo. Quinn accepted the challenge and traveled to Paris to make the film. As always, Quinn was undaunted by the masterful interpretations that preceded him. He managed to view the miserable Quasimodo in a fresh light, emphasizing the special pathos of the hunchback—the pain of the love-besotted creature trapped in a hideous body. The object of the monster's affections, the gypsy Esmeralda, was played by the gorgeous Italian actress Gina Lollabrigida.

The part required Quinn to undergo many hours of elaborate makeup each day before shooting began. To portray the cripple's deformities, Quinn wore a false hump weighing more than 25 pounds, heavy lead weights in his shoes, false teeth, a puttied nose, and steel braces that twisted his body and made the very act of walking seem miraculous all by itself. Both Quinn and Lollabrigida received good notices for the film, but in United States the movie quickly disappeared from the circuit, mostly because of ineffective distribution.

Quinn was one of the most respected and sought-after actors in the world when, on October 11, 1957, newspaper columnist Sheila Graham made a startling announcement: "Anthony Quinn has retired as an actor." The story was true. Quinn had decided to decline all acting offers and focus his talents on directing. His debut as a director would be a remake of *The Buccaneer*, a film Quinn had appeared in years before.

De Mille, whose health was failing, had grown closer to his son-in-law over time and knew that directing was one of his interests. He was revamping *The Buccaneer* as a musical featuring Yul Brynner, the young actor whose performance as the King of Siam in *The King and I* had catapulted him to stardom. De Mille felt the project provided a good opportunity for Quinn to try his hand at directing, and Quinn, who was eager to get this perspective on moviemaking, agreed to work on the film.

In his interview with Sheila Graham, Quinn explained the career move: "After 70 movies, I've had it as an actor. I find directing more exciting, more interesting. I have two more pictures to direct after this [*The Buccaneer*], and it would have to be something fantastically fabulous to make me change my mind once again."

Quinn directed *The Buccaneer* under the close supervision of De Mille, but still his inexperience as a director was evident. The critics were almost uniformly unkind toward Quinn's first directorial effort, and Quinn himself commented on the film's unpopularity: "Our business is the only one in which they demand 50 times their investment, and if they don't get it, it's a flop." Filming *The Buccaneer* cost $5 million, a large sum for the time, and the studio was not at all happy about the low returns. Quinn received scattered praise for his direction of the film's battle scenes, which were spare and to the point, but his debut as a director was far from successful, and Quinn wisely resumed his acting career.

Quinn's return to acting marked the beginning of one of the most satisfying periods of his career. The quality of his roles continued to improve, and his work was honored with awards and critical acclaim. Three roles, virtually back to back, paired Quinn with the leading actresses of the day—Italian stars Anna Magnani and Sophia Loren, and Shirley Booth, an American actress who had received an Oscar in 1954 for her performance in *Come Back Little Sheba.*

Hot Spell, starring Shirley Booth, was the moving story of a man who, after 20 years of marriage, finds he can no longer tolerate his life and flees his family in the company of a teenage girl. The character was difficult to play and extremely unsympathetic, but Quinn managed to make him a heartbreaking example of a man defeated by life and his own weaknesses. In *The Black Orchid*, costarring Sophia Loren, Quinn played the widower-suitor of a widow whose husband had been involved in organized crime. Central to the story is the relationship between the widower and his disapproving daughter.

Quinn and Anna Magnani in Wild Is the Wind, *in which the actor played an Italian immigrant who, soon after his wife's death, attempts a union with his sister-in-law, played by Magnani. Quinn's performance in the film earned him an Oscar nomination for Best Actor.*

It was in *Wild Is the Wind*, however, that Quinn earned the most praise as well as an Academy Award nomination for Best Actor. Directed by the Hollywood great George Cukor, whose films *Dinner at Eight* and *Little Women* are Hollywood classics, *Wild Is the Wind* teamed Quinn with Anna Magnani, known for her explosive acting style and her dynamic performance in Roberto Rossellini's *Open City*. Their fireworks lit up the screen and made for a grandly entertaining spectacle based on a very unusual love story. Quinn plays a proud Italian immigrant who after his wife's death sends for his wife's sister, played by Magnani, to fill the gap in his life. Quinn's intense, deeply subjective style was never so evident as in *Wild Is the Wind*.

When the Oscar nominations for films released during 1957 were announced, Quinn found himself up against Marlon Brando for his film *Sayonara*, Charles Laughton for *Witness for the Prosecution*, Anthony Franciosa for *A Hatful of Rain*, and Alec Guinness for *The Bridge on the River Kwai*. After what must have been painful deliberation, the academy awarded the prize to Guinness for his portrayal of a calculating commander in the epic film about World War II.

Shortly after the awards ceremony, in May 1958, the intrepid television and print journalist Edward R. Murrow paid a visit to the Quinn household and interviewed the entire Quinn family for his television show "Person to Person." It was the first time that the public was allowed to peek into the very private life of the Hollywood family.

Then a fresh crop of westerns beckoned, and Quinn was back in the saddle with a film called *Last Train from Gun Hill*, costarring Kirk Douglas, with whom Quinn had already appeared in three movies. Next came *Warlock*, starring Richard Widmark, Henry Fonda, and Dorothy Malone. In this rather bizarre film, Quinn plays a crippled blond cowboy whose relationship to the character played by Fonda has homosexual undertones. Although Quinn's performance was outstanding, the movie was not a success, perhaps because the subject matter made the audiences of the time a bit uncomfortable.

George Cukor came to Quinn's rescue with a part in his film *Heller in Pink Tights*, starring Sophia Loren as the tenacious Adah Isaacs Menken, an American actress of the Old West whose traveling stage shows provided entertainment for the lonely cowboys out on the range. Quinn played Menken's manager, an inarticulate bumpkin who attempts to straighten out the troupe of haphazard performers. Sophia Loren was making a bid for stardom in the United States and had taken on quite a few curious roles, but in this underrated film she was radiant. *Heller in Pink Tights* was barely noticed despite the two excellent star performances and was never given its due as one of the brightest westerns to come out of that period.

Shortly after, Quinn left the tumbleweeds and stagecoaches behind to star with Lana Turner in *Portrait in Black*, a melodramatic love story dressed in satin and soapsuds. The most interesting aspect of this film was Quinn's on-screen reunion with two of his old

Paramount contract player friends, Anna May Wong and Lloyd Nolan. Quinn was to appear often with Wong, for whom he had a particular fondness, in the late 1950s and early 1960s.

Quinn's next role took him to uncharted territory. In *The Savage Innocents*, he donned the garb of an Eskimo and, as the hunter Inuk, struggled to keep his family alive and the forces of nature at bay. The film was largely silent, and Quinn was forced to make his character believable using little dialogue. Just as he had made a convincing Cheyenne Indian in *The Plainsman* so many years before, Quinn was able to embody the courage and dignity of the Eskimo for whom survival was the only concern.

The advent of the 1960s saw a flurry of activity in Quinn's film career, as well as his return to the stage in one of the most prestigious plays on Broadway at the time. In October 1960, Quinn took on the tremendously difficult role of King Henry in Jean Anouilh's play *Becket*, based on the life of Saint Thomas Becket, chancellor of England and archbishop of Canterbury during the reign of King Henry II. The great English actor Laurence Olivier played Becket, the prelate who was murdered in his own cathedral in 1170 for attempting to protect the Catholic church from corrupting government interests. Becket was subsequently canonized for his strength of will. Quinn has since said of his experience working with Olivier, "Sir Laurence was one of my giants. I took him on in Becket and got slapped down. But it was good for me. I grew, and I'll go on tackling giants all my life."

The play received very good reviews, but in late March the agent Sam Spiegel bought out Quinn's contract to secure Quinn for a part in director David Lean's film spectacular *Lawrence of Arabia*. The movie seemed destined for greatness if only for its remarkable subject. T. E. Lawrence, born in northern Wales in 1888, served as both a soldier and a tactician in the Arab effort to topple the Ottoman Empire just before World War I. He fought in the Arabian deserts, was brutally beaten at the hands of the Turks, and was wounded in combat no less than 32 times. David Lean's Middle Eastern extravaganza is one of the screen's greatest tri-

Quinn as Auda Abu Tayi, the leader of a band of Arab desert warriors, in the David Lean epic Lawrence of Arabia. *Quinn had only a small role in the big-budget extravaganza, but he played it with such power that critics praised his performance as one of the most compelling in the film.*

umphs, and Quinn was mesmerizing as Auda Abu Tayi, the Arab leader of a band of desert warriors who defeat the Turks with the help of Lawrence. Although his role was relatively small, Quinn endowed it with both power and subtlety. Critics took note of Quinn's performance, calling it one of the most compelling in the film.

From the sands of the Sahara, Quinn flew to Greece to play a Greek army officer in *The Guns of Navarone*, director Carl Foreman's adventure classic set on the Aegean island of Navarone. The movie was a huge box-office success, setting new records for ticket sales. As the officer Andrea Stavros, Quinn gave a performance that lifted the film above the level of a mere action feature. Bosley Crowther of the *New York Times* wrote that Quinn's Stavros "has the courage of a lion and the simplicity of a goat," and for such displays of strength and brutishness Quinn has always been known best.

While filming *Guns*, Quinn fell in love with Greece and, after having been made an honorary citizen by an appreciative Greek government, decided to buy some property there. Using the better part of his payment for the movie, Quinn bought two harbors and an isthmus on the island of Rhodes, upon which he intended to build an intellectual hideaway of sorts, catering to actors, painters, and writers. "I will put up a philosophic center for all those who want to come and read and discuss," he said in an interview.

From Greece, Quinn journeyed back to Rome to star in *Barabbas*, a film based on the story of the thief who was pardoned instead of Jesus Christ. Quinn's performance is often credited with saving the picture from disaster; his herculean efforts allowed the essence of the story to shine through the glut of extras and special effects.

The filming of *Barabbas* marked an important departure for Quinn. On the set of the film, Quinn met a young wardrobe mistress named Jolanda Addolori, with whom he began an affair that would rock the tabloids. A scandal erupted when the press discovered the birth of a son to Quinn and Addolori.

Quinn's statement to the press, printed under the headline ANTHONY QUINN ADMITS LOVE CHILD, was straightforward: "The boy is my son, and I am going to acknowledge him. I am not concerned with what people will think as much as with what is good for the boy. I want him to be loved—not to have to go to a

Quinn and Jolanda Addolori, who gave birth to the couple's first son, Francesco, in 1963. Hollywood reporters piled on to criticize Quinn for fathering a child out of wedlock, but he disarmed them with his honesty and his refusal to be shamed or embarrassed by what he considered a joyous event.

psychiatrist at the age of 41 because he wasn't wanted. I am not flaunting what I have done, and I'm not doing anything for anyone's approval, but I'm not giving in to hypocrisy. I want him to have my name. He will have the same love and attention as all my other children."

The tabloids would normally have vilified such indiscreet behavior, but gossip columnists were disarmed by Quinn's refusal to be ashamed and by his principled position. Quinn had Francesco, his first son by Addolori, baptized with his name at St. Peter's Basilica in Rome and arranged divorce proceedings with Katherine, his wife of 27 years. The divorce, on the grounds of mutual incompatibility, became final in 1965, and Quinn married Addolori in January of the following year.

Quinn then returned to the United States to star in *Requiem for a Heavyweight*, one of his finest and most memorable roles. Written by Rod Serling, the creator of the successful television series "The Twilight Zone," *Requiem* had originally been written for television also, but the producers decided to bring it to the big screen.

Quinn was cast as Mountain Rivera, a has-been boxer who bore the scars of every battle he had fought in the ring. The role was a plum for Quinn, who worked painstakingly to endow every scene with power and meaning. However, the attention to detail and the number of takes required to get each scene just right caused friction on the set between the actor and other members of the cast. His costar Jackie Gleason, who played the part of Mountain Rivera's cold-blooded manager, was frustrated by Quinn's methods and complained to the director Ralph Nelson. Aware that Quinn's excruciating perfectionism can be maddening for the cast and crew on a set, Nelson has commented, "Tony has great selfishness as a performer. He thinks how a scene can best serve him. Of course, when he's good he's brilliant, but he just makes it hard for everyone around him." At one point Gleason, infuriated after a particularly unproductive day, threatened to walk off the set and never come back if Quinn persisted in his perfectionist ways.

Quinn and "The Great One," Jackie Gleason, in the 1962 movie Requiem for a Heavyweight. *The two actors respected each other's talents but experienced some tense moments during the filming of* Requiem *as Gleason's patience for Quinn's perfectionist ways sometimes wore thin.*

Quinn's meticulousness may not have won him many friends on the set, but nobody could argue with the result. *Requiem* was a great success due in large part to Quinn's performance, and the critics recognized this. One *New Yorker* critic wrote that in the movie "Quinn looks like one of the greatest actors on earth," and others said that his performance should earn him an Oscar nomination. Also, because *Requiem* wound up being released at the same time as *Barabbas*, the critics had a field day comparing the two characterizations, calling Quinn the "hardest working actor in town." Contrary to the expectations of critics and moviegoers, Quinn was not nominated for an Academy Award that year, but his successes led him to be chosen for another coveted New York stage role.

Tchin-Tchin was originally a French drama, rewritten in 1962 by American author Sidney Michaels as a comedy for the Broadway stage. Quinn starred as a man whose wife had left him for another man, the husband of the character played by the veteran actress Margaret Leighton. Quinn's and Leighton's characters in turn try to find love with each other. Quinn has confessed that he had a great deal of trouble entering the character of Caesario Grimaldi, the scorned husband, saying, "When I understand the character, I become the character. But for me this fellow doesn't exist." Undoubtedly it was hard for a man like Quinn, whose ideas about life and love were never unclear, to empathize with the unfortunate cuckold. Since it was difficult for Quinn to use his usual internal techniques to make Grimaldi come to life, he concentrated instead on the externals, even shaving off a mustache he had grown, in the hope of appearing a more pathetic figure.

Quinn's performance varied widely from night to night. Sometimes *Tchin-Tchin* would be played as a broad comedy, other times as a depressing look at the pain of infidelity. An audience was never sure if it would be treated to belly laughs or tears. But Quinn's career was about to turn yet another corner. Uneven as they were, his performances in *Tschin-Tschin* had caught the attention of a Greek director who could see that the actor was truly an original.

Reflecting on the course of his career, Quinn observed that he enjoyed enormous successes for what seemed like brief periods of time, only to have to prove himself again and again. He once commented, "I'd do something and people would say I was great, and then forget about me. Then in two years it would happen again." He went on to recall an observation made by Elia Kazan, who, according to Quinn, said, "Tony Quinn is always in the process of being discovered."

But Quinn would not ride this roller coaster forever. Of all the characters Quinn portrayed in his career, one role would eventually give Quinn the chance to prove once and for all that he was one of the great actors of his generation.

The British actor Alan Bates joins Quinn for a dance in Zorba the Greek. *In the 1964 blockbuster, based on the Nikos Kazantzakis novel of the same name, Quinn played Alexis "Epidemic" Zorba, a middle-aged Greek peasant with a passionate spirit and an extraordinary lust for life.*

CHAPTER SEVEN

Zorba the Star

Based on the novel by Nikos Kazantzakis, *Zorba the Greek* had been a tough sell so far in Hollywood; despite the popularity of the novel, nearly all the top Hollywood actors whom the director Michael Cacoyannis approached had shown little interest in the movie script. Quinn has talked about the difficulties the director had finding someone to play Zorba: "Nobody wanted to do it. Burl Ives turned it down. So did Burt Lancaster. They said, 'Who cares about an old man making love to a broken-down old broad?'" But when Cacoyannis approached Quinn with the script for *Zorba the Greek*, the actor knew instinctively that Zorba—the feisty, middle-aged Greek whose appetite for life is exceeded only by his thirst for love—was the role of a lifetime.

The story of *Zorba the Greek* revolved around a budding friendship between a young British writer, played by Alan Bates, and Alexis "Epidemic" Zorba ("Epidemic" because, as Zorba explains, "everywhere I go people say I louse things up") on the Greek island of Crete. An important subplot featured Zorba's romantic involve-

Irene Papas plants a tender kiss on Quinn's bristly cheek in Zorba the Greek, *which received seven Oscar nominations in 1965, including Quinn's for Best Actor. When Quinn did not win the award, some observers suggested that it was because the academy disapproved of his personal life.*

ment with a middle-aged former prostitute, played by the French actress Lila Kedrova, who learned English while on the set.

The financing for *Zorba the Greek* was limited, and the movie would have to be produced on a very low budget. Instead of receiving a salary and a lump sum on signing, the actors were to be paid a percentage of the movie's gross revenues. Quinn's percentage would be one-third. Because of the shortage of funds, there was some doubt whether the movie would ever be made, and even after the filming of *Zorba* was under way money was a constant worry. The completion of the project was uncertain even during the last weeks of production. At one point, Quinn had to use his influence with Hollywood investors to get additional financing. Eventually the movie was completed.

Zorba was a smash at the box office as well as with the critics. *Time* magazine heralded the film as "a grand, uproarious bacchanalian bash," and the *New York Times* gushed, "He is Adam in the garden of Eden, Odysseus on the windy plains of Troy." It was no surprise to anyone that his performance in *Zorba* would snag Quinn a second Oscar nomination for best actor in 1964.

Once again, however, the Oscar eluded Quinn when the big night rolled around. While *Zorba* won for best black-and-white cinematography and Lila Kedrova was honored with an Oscar for Best Supporting Actress, Quinn was passed over in favor of Rex Harrison, who won for his starring role as Henry Higgins in *My Fair Lady*. There were those who believed that Quinn had been snubbed because of his recent and highly publicized affair with Jolanda Addolori. Columnist Marilyn Beck wrote, "Many flicker folk believe Anthony Quinn lost to Harrison because of his personal life. They think Tony's admission of siring two families simultaneously outraged the industry's moral code and this negated his brilliant acting job in *Zorba*."

There was precedent for such snubbing by the academy. For example, Ingrid Bergman had been virtually hounded out of Hollywood during the late 1940s for her relationship with Italian director Roberto Rossellini and for bearing his child out of wedlock. It may have been the progressive 1960s, but Quinn had clearly ruffled the feathers of more than a few traditionalists with his unconventional personal life.

During the filming of Zorba, *Quinn took time off the set to visit the CARE Children's Center in Chania, Crete, and romp with the orphans in residence there. During his visit the actor was treated to a program of Greek music and dance by the children.*

The academy's decision had no effect on the steady stream of glowing reviews that came pouring in, nor on Quinn's popularity, which had risen to new heights. In fact, *Zorba* was so successful that Quinn would later admit to feeling almost sorry that the performance had so overshadowed his previous award-winning roles in *Lust for Life* and *Viva Zapata!* It was becoming increasingly clear that Quinn's portrayal of Zorba would be the yardstick against which all of his subsequent performances would be measured.

Around this time, Quinn was becoming more and more interested in politics, giving special attention to the civil rights movement that was sweeping the United States. Having been denied leading roles and cast almost exclusively in ethnic parts for so many years, Quinn had experienced the evils of racism firsthand and was eager to lend his support in the struggle for civil rights. In August 1963, he took part in a petition drive to expedite the passing of the civil rights bill then before Congress. Other petitioners included the author James Baldwin, best known for his book *The Fire Next Time*; James Jones, author of *From Here to Eternity*; and concert pianist Hazel Scott.

Quinn, who now made about half a million dollars per picture, made three movies in quick succession after *Zorba*. The first was *Behold a Pale Horse*, a 1964 film that tells the tale of a Spanish police commander who lures an old enemy out of hiding in the French Pyrenees in the aftermath of the Spanish Civil War. In the second movie, *The Visit*, Quinn played the former lothario of the world's richest woman, who is busily seeking revenge on him for having disgraced her. Then Quinn immersed himself in an international production called *La Fabuleuse Aventure de Marco Polo*, in which he played the Mongol warrior and chieftain Kublai Khan.

During the late 1960s, commitments to various film projects demanded that Quinn travel constantly, and he did so with his new family in tow. He starred in a French-Yugoslavian production called *The 25th Hour*; a film called *The Rover*, which was filmed in Italy; *Guns for San Sebastian*, an adventure movie filmed in Mexico; and

The Magus, based on the novel by John Fowles and filmed on the Spanish island of Majorca.

The film *The Shoes of the Fisherman,* in which Quinn plays a Russian-born political prisoner who eventually becomes the head of the Roman Catholic church, presented a unique challenge for Quinn, who looked back on playing the Vatican chief: "I was in great conflict with myself. I literally went through a psychosomatic experience and was in the hospital for three weeks. I finally went to director Michael Anderson and asked him 'How in hell do you play a saint?' He told me, 'A saint is only a man who is competing with God, not his fellow man.'" The director's words helped clarify the role for Quinn, who in his 1957 Oscar acceptance speech had described his approach to his own work in much the same terms.

In The Shoes of the Fisherman, *Quinn plays a Roman Catholic bishop who, after spending 20 years in a Siberian work camp, climbs through the ranks of the Vatican to become the first Russian pope. Laurence Olivier and John Gielgud also appeared in the film, which was shot mostly in Rome.*

When asked about his preparation for the role, Quinn said, "In considering Pope Kiril, I thought, among other things, of how he'd been working in the Siberian mines and how he would look, dressed in white, in a color film. The white cassock would have made a heavy me look like an elephant, and I had to go way down for that one. When I act, I feel the character's weight is important to me. Don't ask me why, but when I played Kiril, I thought he should weigh 187 pounds, and in playing the pope, I learned the tremendous importance of mind over matter."

Filmed mostly in Rome, *The Shoes of the Fisherman* used sets that were specially constructed in the Cinecetta Studios to look exactly like the Vatican complex. Because Quinn had himself been raised a Roman Catholic, he was familiar with the intricate rituals of Catholicism, and his Pope Kiril seemed perfectly natural. But even so, *The Shoes of the Fisherman* was a financial failure, perhaps because audiences had grown accustomed to and preferred Quinn in the less refined roles he usually played.

In his next major film, *The Secret of Santa Vittoria*, Quinn played the slightly foolish and unkempt Italo Bombolini and was reunited with Anna Magnani, who played Bombolini's wife, Rosa. Quinn and Magnani played off each other's idiosyncrasies, as they always had, to create humor and bittersweet pathos in the story of a town that hides a vast supply of wine from an invading Nazi army regiment during World War II.

Quinn has said of playing the part, "I've known many Bombolinis in Italy. The whole key to his character is he has to fool everybody. I've lived in Italy for many years, and I know the Italian people well. They seldom give you a straight answer. . . . It's part of their charm and the secret of their phenomenal ability to survive. They never commit themselves; they go along with whatever they think you want them to do. That's why they've lost every war—but won every peace." Quinn's ability to play such drastically different roles in succession, switching from the austere Pope Kiril to the bumbling Italo Bombolini, is a testament to his great talent as a character actor.

Quinn returned to the United States in 1969 and in June of that year was invited to cast his handprint in cement outside Grauman's Chinese Theater in Los Angeles. Quinn happily accepted the honor and became the 155th Hollywood celebrity to do so. The handprints are a source of delight to movie fans who visit the theater in droves to place their own hands in the casts made by such Hollywood legends as Marilyn Monroe and Errol Flynn.

One year after the death of Martin Luther King, Jr., who was assassinated in 1968, Quinn helped narrate a documentary, directed by Sidney Lumet and Joseph L. Mankiewicz, about the civil rights leader's life and times. Entitled *King: A Filmed Record . . . Montgomery to Memphis*, the film also documented the progress of the civil rights movement from the acts of civil disobedience and organized marches of the 1950s and early 1960s to King's assassination in Tennessee at the age of 39.

During the early 1970s, Quinn was involved in numerous television projects. These included a variety show that he hosted with the singer Peggy Lee, a television series called "The City," and an appearance on "The Dick Cavett Show."

In his interview with Cavett, Quinn sparked a minor controversy when he mentioned his desire to make a film based on the life of Henri Christophe, the black leader of the 1803 revolution in Haiti that led to that country's independence, and stated that he intended to play the starring part of Christophe himself. For these remarks, critics accused Quinn of being insensitive to the plight of black actors, who would rarely if ever be cast in nonwhite roles, effectively cutting them off from much of the available work. In an open letter on this issue in the *New York Times* one writer came down heavily on Quinn, and the actor responded in a letter of his own, saying, "Why do you want to relegate me to playing Mexican bandits and redskins who bite the dust? Why can't I play a pope, or an

Eskimo, an Indian, a Greek, an Italian—any part where I can make a statement about my life and time? I know the dangerous terrain I am invading. I have all the qualms any artist has before a blank piece of canvas. It's more fearful than facing a bull in the ring." Apparently some avenues were off limits to the man who had portrayed Arabs, Mongols, Chinese, and others for the major portion of his career—the film was never made.

More astute critics were aware of Quinn's understanding of the problems faced by minorities in the United States and his longtime commitment to civil rights. This commitment continued during the 1970s, as evidenced by a documentary film Quinn made during this period. The film, *Voice of La Raza*, was a candid report from Spanish-speaking Americans on the problems they had experienced with discrimination and racism. To make the film, Quinn traveled across the United States, visiting the Hispanic neighborhoods of New York City and Los Angeles to meet and talk to the people who lived there.

Following the foray into television and documentary film, Quinn returned to character acting, but he continued to take on various other challenges. One such challenge was the writing of an autobiography. Entitled *The Original Sin*, the book, which was published in 1972, covered the early years of Quinn's life, up until the age of 21. When asked by an interviewer why he had only written about his youth, Quinn exclaimed, "Why not? By then I had been in the Mexican Revolution, boxed Primo Carnera, did a play with Mae West, impressed John Barrymore, preached with Aimee Semple MacPherson, got drunk with Thomas Wolfe, traveled with Jim Tully and sang with Chaliapin!" *The Original Sin* received good reviews, and Quinn was complimented on his lively writing style. Robert Berkvist of the *New York Times Book Review* wrote, "Quinn has given us the story of his psychoanalysis, and through it, if not the story of his life, at least the roots of a marvelous tale that would do credit to any storyteller."

Director Moustapha Akkad discusses a scene with Quinn on the set of Mohammed, Messenger of God, *a dramatization of the events surrounding the founding of the Muslim faith. The film created a stir when Islamic fundamentalists objected to the portrayal of the prophet Mohammed.*

During the 1970s, Quinn took on fewer film projects, but one project embroiled him in yet another controversy. The film *Mohammed, Messenger of God*, was the story of Mohammed, the founder of the Muslim faith, or Islam. Although the script was written from the point of view of Mohammed's uncle Hamza, played by Quinn, the movie incited a furious controversy because Muslim belief strictly forbids any visual representation of Mohammed. So intense was the furor over *Mohammed* that at one point a group of terrorists held employees of the Washington, D.C., office of the Jewish organization B'nai Brith hostage in an attempt to force the cancellation of the film's premiere. Eventually the standoff ended peacefully, and *Mohammed, Messenger of God* was widely released in the United States.

Quinn seemed unbothered by the controversy surrounding *Mohammed*. In fact, throughout his career Quinn remained unafraid of taking risks, and he understood that controversy and bad reviews had to be expected along the way. He was more concerned with his own artistic development than with the opinions of the critics. This approach would carry him into the 1980s and beyond.

Quinn proudly displays his Golden Globe Award, which he won in 1987. The special achievement award—named after his onetime father-in-law, Cecil B. De Mille—was presented to Quinn in recognition of a lifetime of outstanding contributions to the cinematic arts.

CHAPTER EIGHT

A Man of His Own Creation

Quinn's biggest film of 1981 was *Lion of the Desert*, a sweeping, $30 million epic. The film was modeled after director David Lean's sandy opus *Lawrence of Arabia*, and the Syrian-born director of *Lion*, Moustapha Akkad, even hired Maurice Jarre, the same composer Lean had used to compose the score for his movie.

Quinn played Omar Mukhtar, a heroic Arab schoolteacher who fights to defend his country against an invasion from Italian forces during World War II. The cast also included Rod Steiger as Benito Mussolini and Oliver Reed as a Fascist general. The film critic David Denby called the film "an inspirational epic for Third World audiences" and went on to say that "Quinn looks marvelous on his white stallion, calmly reading the Koran while the Italian tanks follow in hot pursuit."

The following year, Quinn presented his paintings and sculptures in an exhibition at the Center Art Galleries in Honolulu,

Hawaii. While Quinn had contributed paintings to other exhibitions for many years, this was his first one-man show, and he was surprised and pleased by its popularity. The gallery displayed more than 65 pieces, with special attention given to a group of sculptural forms in wood and marble called "Anthony Quinn's Women." The show was a remarkable success, and every piece was sold, bringing Quinn the handsome sum of nearly $2 million. But the money was not the most important issue for Quinn, who commented after the exhibition, "Without art, there is no reason for living. I'd just be an animal if I didn't create some form of life."

But the siren song of the performing arts was again calling Quinn, and instead of following up his first triumph with another show of paintings, he returned to moviemaking. The 1983 film *Valentina* explored the relationship between an elderly priest, played by Quinn, and a teenage boy who seeks his guidance. *Valentina* was filmed in Spain, in the Spanish language.

Quinn then returned to the stage in one of his favorite roles—Zorba. *Zorba, the Musical,* like the play on which it is based, was directed by Michael Cacoyannis and was an enormous success, delighting audiences and playing to sold-out houses night after night for three years. After opening in Philadelphia, *Zorba* toured five cities, eventually making its way to Broadway, where it finished its run in 1986. Quinn said of his by then trademark performances, "Today I'm a better Zorba. Before, I had to paint my hair white. Now I'm just right." And the audiences who flocked to see Quinn sing and dance his way through the bittersweet story clearly agreed.

But even with the heavy commitment of daily stage performances, Quinn still found time to pursue his art and myriad other undertakings. One of these projects was the second volume of his autobiography, the follow-up to *Original Sin,* called *Suddenly Sunset,* taking up where the first autobiography left off, tracing the course of events in Quinn's life from age 21 on.

Of all the praise and prizes won by Quinn in his career, one honor that meant a great deal to him was that presented by his hometown. The Belevedere Library in East Los Angeles stood on the site of Anthony Quinn's boyhood home, and though his family's little shack was long gone, the area held many memories for him. On July 11, 1983, Los Angeles County hailed Quinn by rededicating the Belevedere Library and changing its name to the Anthony Quinn Library. In a highly emotional speech, Quinn graciously accepted the tribute, saying, "The home I used to live in used to be located right here on this parking lot. I want to tell you without crying because I lost the man I loved most in the whole world right here—my father died in a car accident on this corner."

Quinn gave large portions of his speech in Spanish for the benefit of the largely Hispanic audience who turned out to admire their hero in person. Quinn continued, "I remember how difficult it was and how far away we had to go to find books. . . . They were the only friends we had. My father believed the only answer to prejudice and negativism was knowledge, and I firmly agree with him." The library's officials accepted Quinn's gift of a six-foot-tall bronze sculpture, as well as many of his own rare books, paintings, sculptures, and manuscripts.

In 1984, Quinn again made news, but in quite an unexpected way. With the contribution of an abstract oil painting, Quinn joined the ranks of artists and artisans who had made their mark in the world of postal stamps. The painting was made into a lithographic series to be sold in limited quantities and used as the cover art for the program created by the World Federation of United Nations Associations (WFUNA), to celebrate the new "Flag Series" of postal stamps.

In 1988, Quinn extended the break he had taken from movie-making in order to write reviews for the British magazine *New Statesman and Society*, a highly respected publication covering politics, religion, and the arts. Quinn chose difficult material to review, such as Richard Ellman's weighty biography of the 19th-century playwright Oscar Wilde, American writer John Updike's novel *Rabbit at Rest*, and the works of British humorist Kingsley Amis, who is a personal favorite of Quinn's.

In October of that year, *Stamps* magazine reported that Quinn had created another painting for WFUNA's limited lithograph series, this time depicting the faces of a man and a woman. The artwork, created exclusively to commemorate the 40th anniversary of the Universal Declaration of Human Rights, made Quinn a respected figure in the art world.

In 1990, Quinn resumed his movie and television career with no less than five projects, two for television and three for the big screen. In the film *Revenge*, Quinn was cast as an aging but still extremely powerful and wealthy man married to a much younger woman, played by actress Madeline Stowe, who has an affair with a man played by Kevin Costner. Ralph Novack, film critic for *People* magazine, wrote, "Quinn, as Stowe's husband, is magnificent. The aging cuckold is no new role, but he oozes stubborness, pride, and an odd sense of honor. This may be his best role since *A Dream of Kings*."

Anthony Quinn's thespian son, Francesco, appears in 1984 with Maria Teresa Relin in the Franco Rosi film Quo Vadis, *shot in Yugoslavia. In another acting role, Francesco Quinn played alongside his father and sister Valentina in* The Old Man and the Sea.

Lorenzo Quinn graduates from New York University in 1988. Born in May 1966, he was Anthony and Jolanda Quinn's third child.

Quinn then returned to television for the first time in almost 20 years to make *The Old Man and the Sea*, a project based on the Ernest Hemingway novel of the same name. Quinn played Santiago, the aged fisherman whose battle to catch an enormous marlin is the focal point of the story of determination and will. Two of Quinn's children, his son Francesco and daughter Valentina, were featured alongside their father in supporting roles. The television movie earned enthusiastic reviews for Quinn's performance. For example, the critic David Hiltbrand wrote, "No matter what the rest of this t.v. year brings, you'll see nothing like the mighty Quinn."

During the arduous filming of *The Old Man and the Sea*, Quinn began experiencing chest pains. The discomfort did not keep him from meeting a rigorous production schedule of 10-hour days shooting on the open sea of the Caribbean, but a subsequent visit to the doctor confirmed that he had a heart condition. After undergoing open-heart surgery, Quinn went back to work. When asked by an amazed interviewer why he insisted on continuing to work so hard, Quinn said with a laugh, "To me work is something physical, like digging ditches. Acting, writing, painting, sculpting is child's play. It's not very hard work kissing Bo Derek!"

Quinn returned to television for *Knockout: Hollywood's Love Affair with Boxing*, a look at some of the greatest boxing films of all time. He took part as an on-screen narrator for the program, which showed actual boxing footage of heavyweight champions such as Muhammad Ali and Joe Louis as well as clips from films such as *Rocky, Somebody Up There Likes Me, Raging Bull,* and Quinn's own *Requiem for a Heavyweight.*

Quinn and director Spike Lee at the Cannes Film Festival in 1991. In Lee's Jungle Fever, *Quinn plays an Italian-American widower who incessantly burdens his son with guilt. In the darkly comic role, Quinn proves once more that he is a master of his craft.*

Toward the end of 1990, Quinn began working on a high-profile project written and directed by Spike Lee, creator of *Do the Right Thing* and *Mo' Better Blues*. Like Lee's other films, his newest, called *Jungle Fever*, was as skillfully made as it was controversial. *Jungle Fever* tells the story of a young black architect who becomes involved with an Italian-American secretary. Quinn plays the ailing father of a gentle Bensonhurst shopowner who is driven out of the house by his father's bitterness and anguish. Quinn, as the angry old man who lives only in the past and subjects his son and himself to endless mental and emotional torture, turns in a brilliant performance. Had another actor delivered such a powerful performance, it would not have gone unnoticed, but at this point in his career Quinn was expected to deliver nothing less than brilliance, so when he did, little mention was made of it.

Three more film projects engaged Quinn in 1991 in both supporting and starring parts. The first was *Only the Lonely*, starring John Candy, Ally Sheedy, and Maureen O'Hara, an old friend of Quinn's from his early days in Hollywood. Next were *Mobsters*, starring Christian Slater, and *Star for Two*, the latter teaming Quinn with an old friend, Lauren Bacall.

The hectic film schedule Quinn kept would no doubt have exhausted most actors much younger than Quinn, who even in his late seventies showed no sign of slowing down. Quinn himself provided fans with a clue to his motivation and incredible drive: "I act for the same reasons, to a great extent, that Gauguin painted and Mountain [Rivera, his character in *Requiem for a Heavyweight*] fought. . . . When I was a kid I had illusions about what the world should be like and a sense of beauty that has not been verified by my experience. I act because I envision a better world . . . and selfishly . . . because I, too, want to be somebody."

Selected Filmography

1956	*The Hunchback of Notre Dame* Paris Films
1961	*The Guns of Navarone* Columbia
1962	*Lawrence of Arabia* Columbia/Horizon
1962	*Barabbas* Columbia
1962	*Requiem for a Heavyweight* Columbia
1964	*Zorba the Greek* 20th Century Fox
1978	*The Greek Tycoon* Universal
1981	*Lion of the Desert* Falcon International
1988	*Revenge* Columbia
1990	*Jungle Fever* Universal
1991	*Only the Lonely* 20th Century Fox
1991	*Mobsters* Universal

Chronology

1915	Anthony Rudolph Oaxaca Quinn is born in Chihuahua, Mexico, on April 21
1920	Quinn family moves to East Los Angeles
1926	Frank Quinn is hit by a car and killed on January 10
1929	Anthony Quinn meets Aimee Semple McPherson and becomes a member of her organization, Foursquare Gospel Church
1934	Appears in Mae West's production of *Clean Beds*; meets John Barrymore
1936	Quinn plays the part of a convict in his first film, *Parole!*; is cast by director Cecil B. De Mille in *The Plainsman*, his first featured part; meets Katherine De Mille, adopted daughter of Cecil B. De Mille
1937	Marries Katherine De Mille on October 21; signs contract with Paramount Studios
1939	Makes his third and last movie with Cecil B. De Mille; his son Christopher is born

1941	Christopher Quinn drowns in a pool on the estate of the comedian W. C. Fields on March 15; Quinn's first daughter, Christina, is born; Quinn stars with Errol Flynn in the movie *They Died with Their Boots On*
1942	Kathleen Quinn is born
1943	Quinn is cast in the movie *The Ox-Bow Incident* with Dana Andrews and Francis Ford, a film that would be considered one of the finest in his career and one that became a modern classic
1945	Duncan Quinn is born
1946	Quinn signs up with Warner Bros. Studios
1947	Appears on Broadway in *The Gentleman from Athens*
1948	Plays Stanley Kowalski in the Tennessee Williams play *A Streetcar Named Desire*; makes his television debut in *Pride's Castle*
1952	Valentina Quinn is born; Quinn makes *Viva Zapata!*
1953	Wins an Oscar for Best Supporting Actor, for his role as Eufemio Zapata in *Viva Zapata!*; moves to Italy
1954	Quinn plays the strongman Zampano in Federico Fellini's *La Strada*; plays Paul Gauguin in *Lust For Life*, winning a second Oscar for Best Supporting Actor

1956	Stars in *The Hunchback of Notre Dame*
1957	Directs *The Buccaneer*
1962	Appears in *Lawrence of Arabia* and *Barabbas*; meets Jolanda Addolori; stars in *Requiem for a Heavyweight*
1963	Son Francesco is born
1964	Quinn plays Alexis "Epidemic" Zorba in *Zorba the Greek*, for which he is nominated for an Oscar (Best Actor), son Danny is born
1965	Divorces Katherine De Mille
1966	Marries Jolanda Addolori; son Lorenzo is born
1969	Quinn returns to the United States; in June becomes the 155th star to cast his handprints in concrete outside Grauman's Chinese Theater in Hollywood
1972	The first installment of Quinn's auto-biography, *The Original Sin*, is published
1981	Quinn is cast in *Lion of the Desert*
1982	Has his first major show of oil paintings and sculpture in Honolulu, Hawaii
1983	Reprises the role of Zorba on Broadway; appears in the Spanish film *Valentina*; the Belevedere Library in East Los Angeles is renamed the Anthony Quinn Library

1984   Quinn creates a limited-edition lithograph
                        for the World Federation of United Nations
                        Associations (WFUNA)

1988   Contributes book reviews to the British
                        magazine *New Statesman and Society*

1990   Stars in *The Old Man and the Sea*, which also
                        featured his son Francisco and daughter
                        Valentina in supporting roles; undergoes
                        open-heart surgery; stars in *Revenge* with
                        Kevin Costner

1991–92   Is involved in a flurry of film projects,
                        including *Only the Lonely* with John Candy,
                        Mobsters with Christian Slater, and the Spike
                        Lee film *Jungle Fever*; continues to paint
                        and sculpt; makes occasional television
                        appearances; wins Hispanics of Achievement
                        Award for his artistic contributions to the
                        entertainment industry

Further Reading

Bawden, Liz-Anne, ed. *Oxford Companion to Film*. New York: Oxford University Press, 1976.

Bona, Damon, and Mason Wiley. *Inside Oscar: The Unofficial History of the Academy Awards*. New York: Ballantine Books, 1985.

Hadley-Garcia, George. *Hispanic Hollywood*. New York: Citadel, 1990.

Hall, Lorrie. *Strasberg's Method, As Taught by Lorrie Hall*. Woodbridge, CT: Ox Bow Publishing, 1985.

MacBean, James R. *Film & Revolution*. Bloomington: Indiana University Press, 1976.

Michael, Paul. *The Academy Awards, 1927–1982*. New York: Crown, 1982.

Ragan, John David. *Emiliano Zapata*. New York: Chelsea House, 1989.

Sennett, Ted. *Great Hollywood Movies*. New York: Abrams, 1983.

Index

PICTURE CREDITS

Courtesy of the Academy of Motion Picture Arts and Sciences: pp. 17, 28, 33; The Bettmann Archive: pp. 14, 20, 25, 30, 32, 34, 40, 42, 44, 45, 48, 52, 55, 58, 59, 60, 63, 69, 74, 76, 83; Library of Congress: p. 22; Reuters/Bettmann: p. 90; Springer/Bettmann Film Archive: pp. 36, 50; UPI/Bettmann: pp. 18, 24, 26, 38, 41, 56, 66, 70, 72, 77, 79, 84, 88, 89

MELISSA AMDUR is a New York–based writer with interests ranging from economics to art history. She has worked as an editor in book and magazine publishing, has traveled widely, and is also the author of *Linda Ronstadt* in the Chelsea House series HISPANICS OF ACHIEVEMENT.

RODOLFO CARDONA is professor of Spanish and comparative literature at Boston University. A renowned scholar, he has written many works of criticism, including *Ramón, a Study of Gómez de la Serna and His Works* and *Visión del esperpento: Teoría y práctica del esperpento en Valle-Inclán.* Born in San José, Costa Rica, he earned his B.A. and M.A. from Louisiana State University and received a Ph.D. from the University of Washington. He has taught at Case Western Reserve University, the University of Pittsburgh, the University of Texas at Austin, the University of New Mexico, and Harvard University.

JAMES COCKCROFT is currently a visiting professor of Latin American and Caribbean studies at the State University of New York at Albany. A three-time Fulbright scholar, he earned a Ph.D. from Stanford University and has taught at the University of Massachusetts, the University of Vermont, and the University of Connecticut. He is the author or coauthor of numerous books on Latin American subjects, including *Neighbors in Turmoil: Latin America, The Hispanic Experience in the United States: Contemporary Issues and Perspectives,* and *Outlaws in the Promised Land: Mexican Immigrant Workers and America's Future.*